Butterfly Spheres

Butterfly Spheres

by

Lissalei

One-Off Press
Prescott, Arizona
2009

Many of the following images contain pieces by, amongst others, Aubrey Beardsley (page 33), John Anster Fitzgerald (page 24, left), John William Godward (pages 21, 24 right, 25, 26, 38, 40), Gustav Klimt (page 12), and Alphonse Mucha (page 14). Lissalei's intent is to revisit, recast, and recycle work that is today seen more as cliché than exciting and new as it once was. "I hope they would forgive me for all the changes—some small, some quite large—that I've done to their work," Lissalei. Their works are in public domain by reason of publication dates and when the artists died.

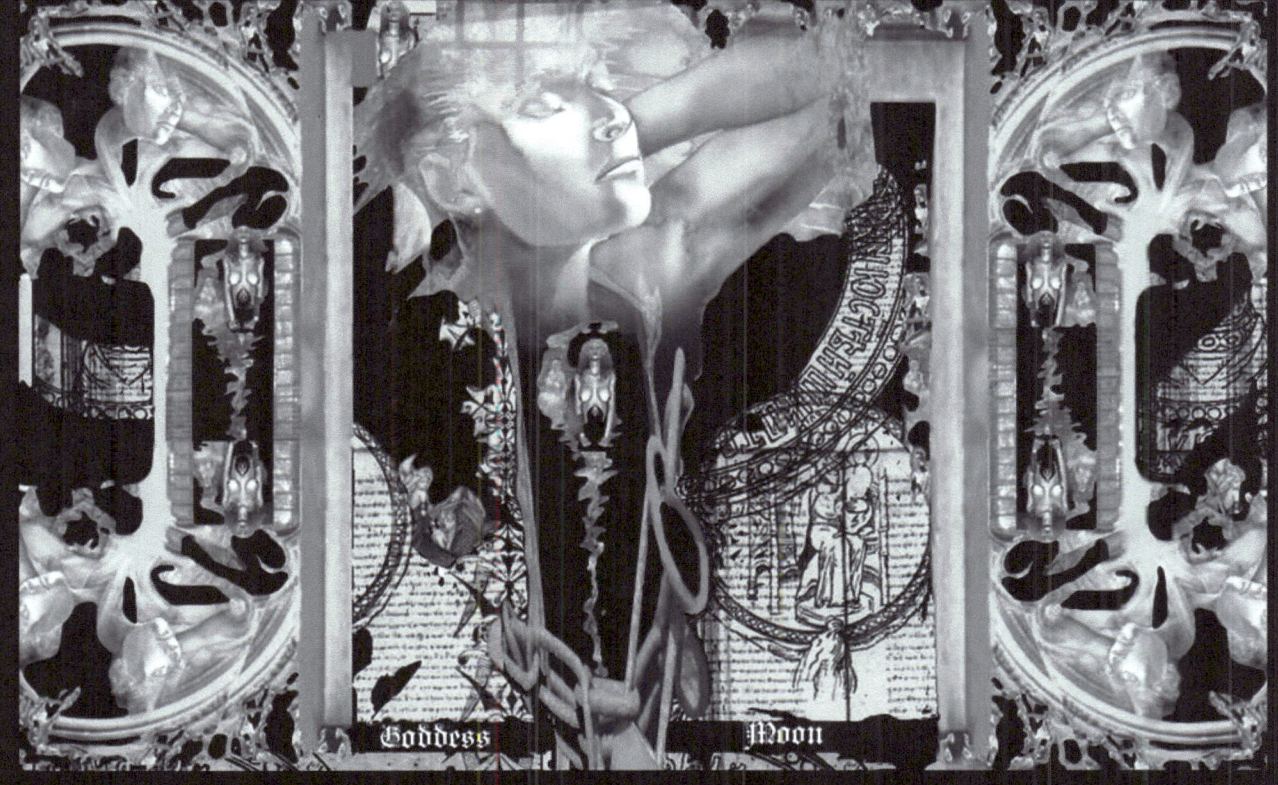

Goddess   Moon

Chill wet wind
knifes through barren branches
A soul shivers
But carried
   A dark light
      A warm cold
         A world apart

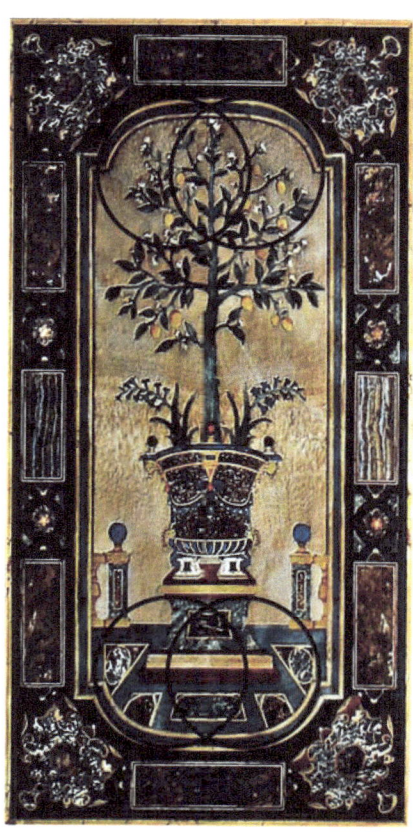 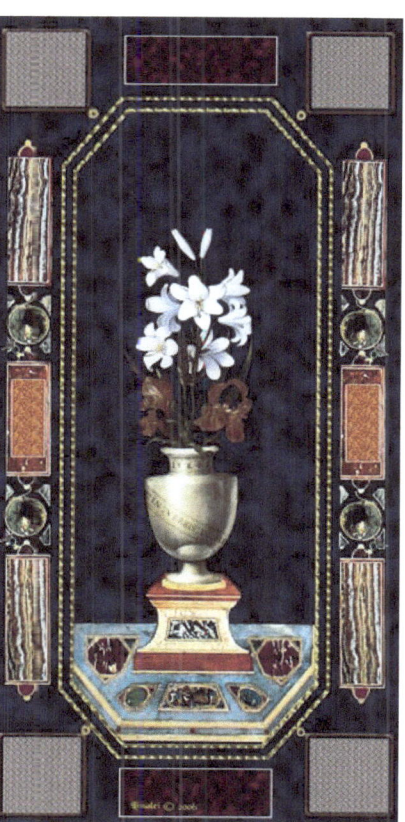 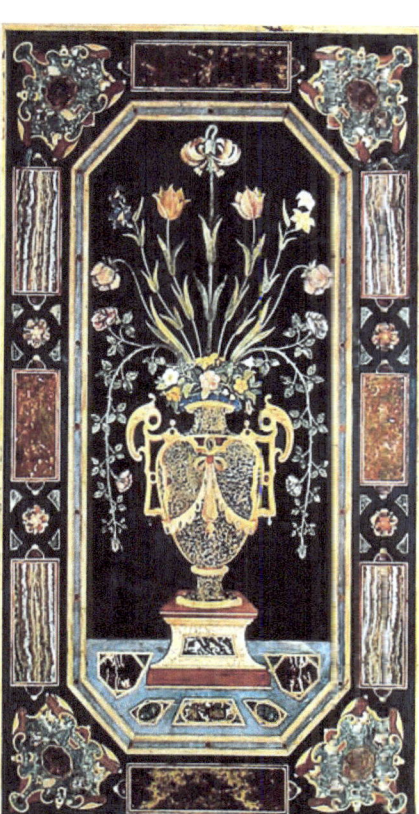

Triptych (mixed media)

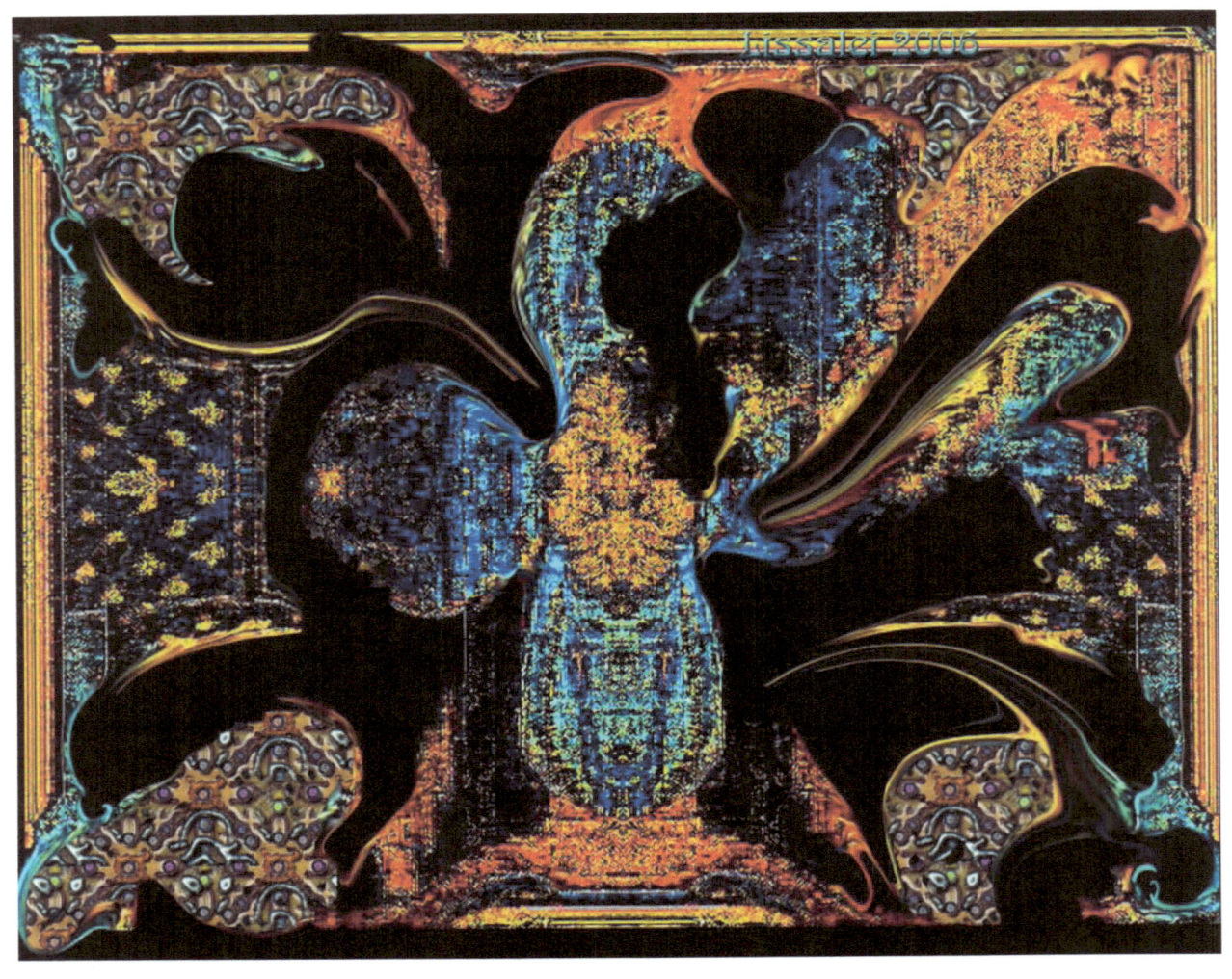

Erosion

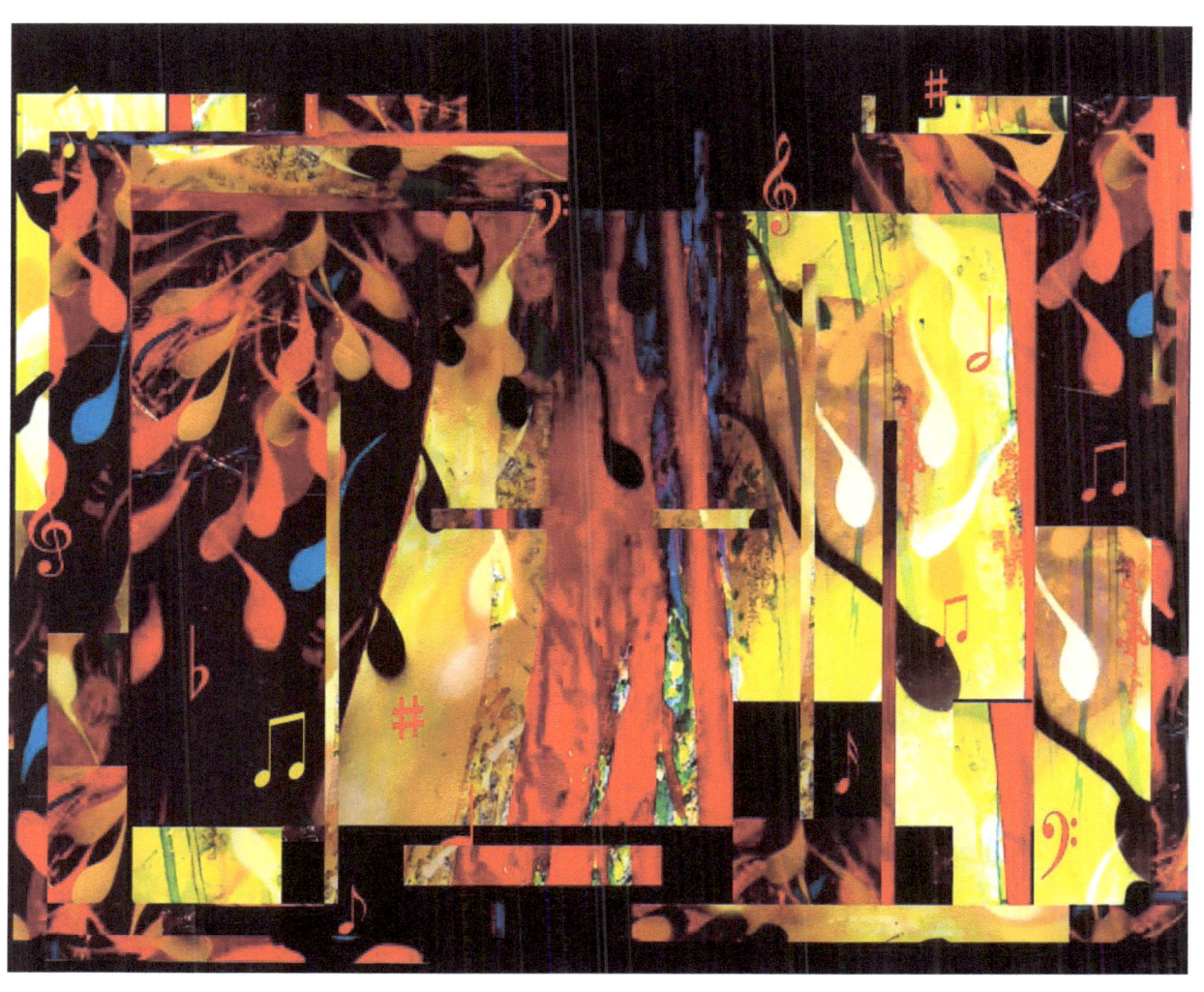

The Color of Music

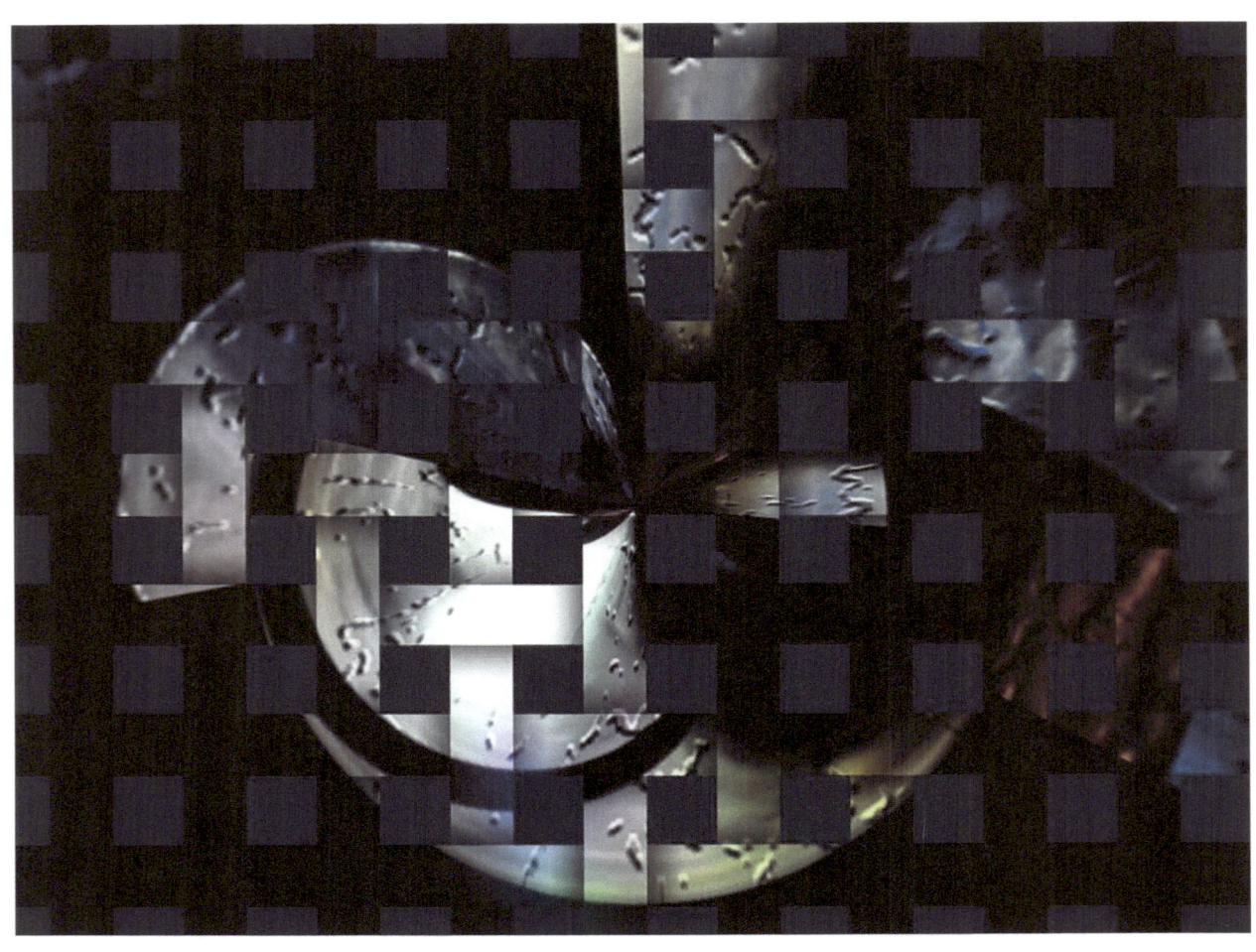

Masked

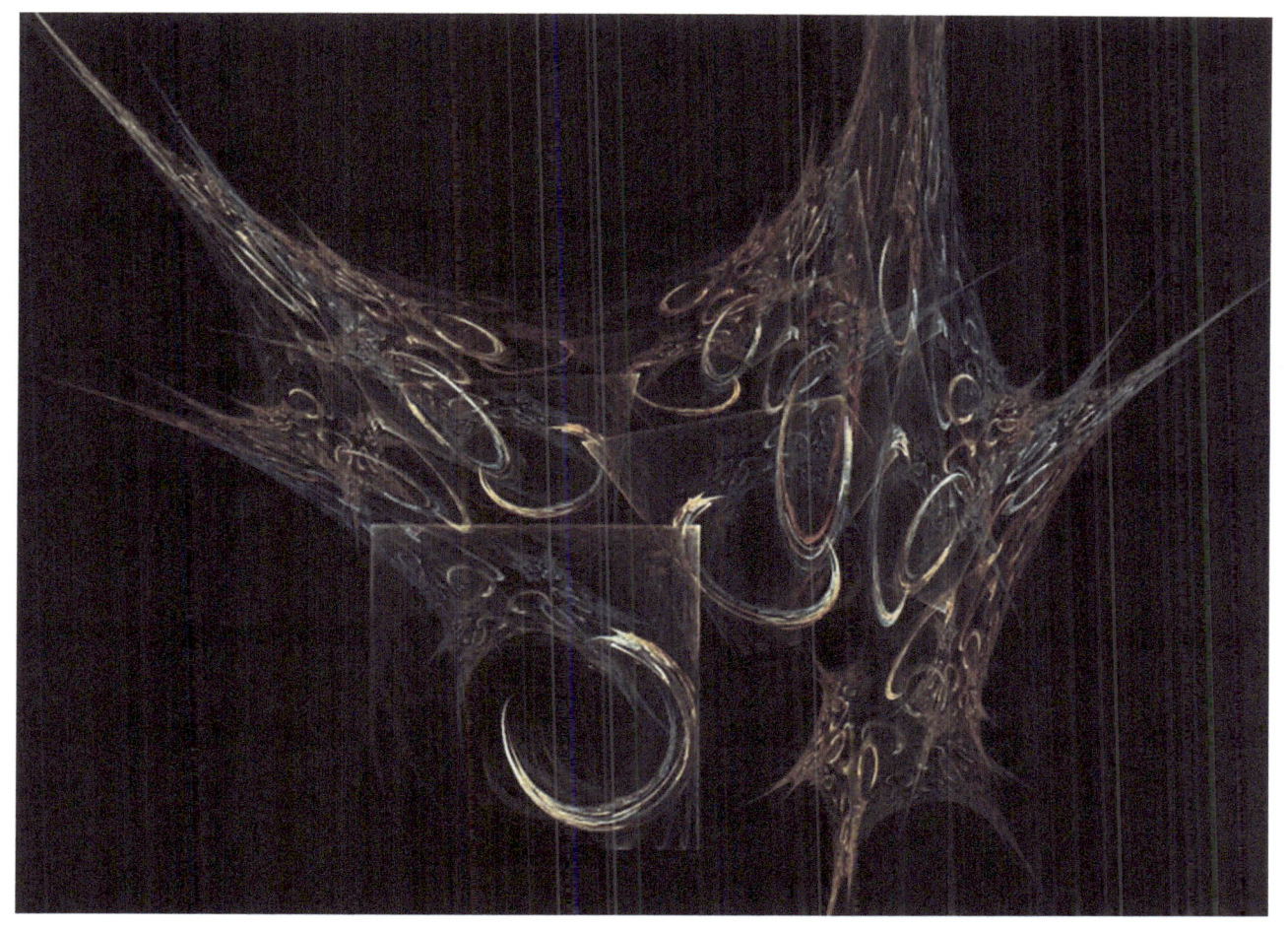

Links

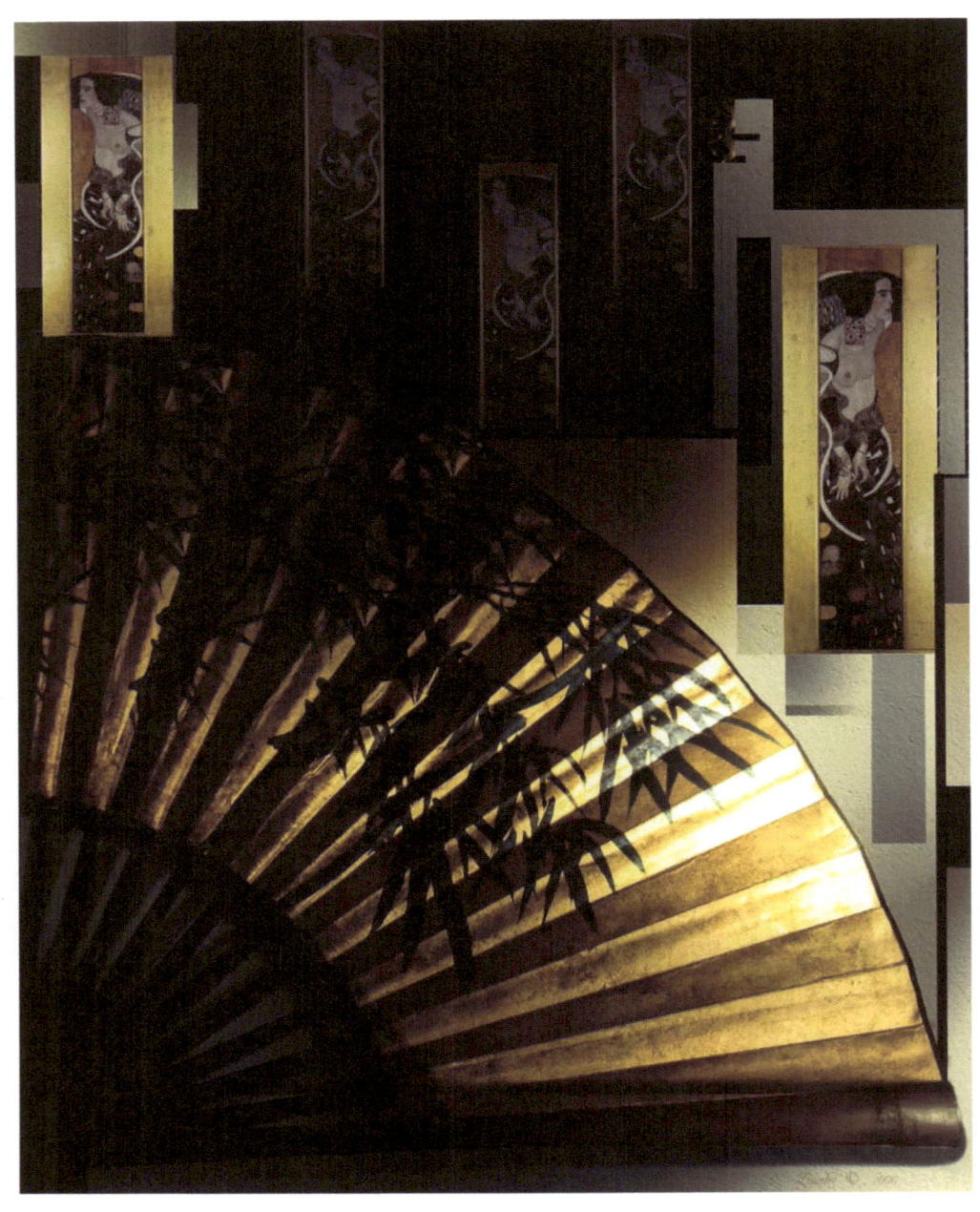

Fandango

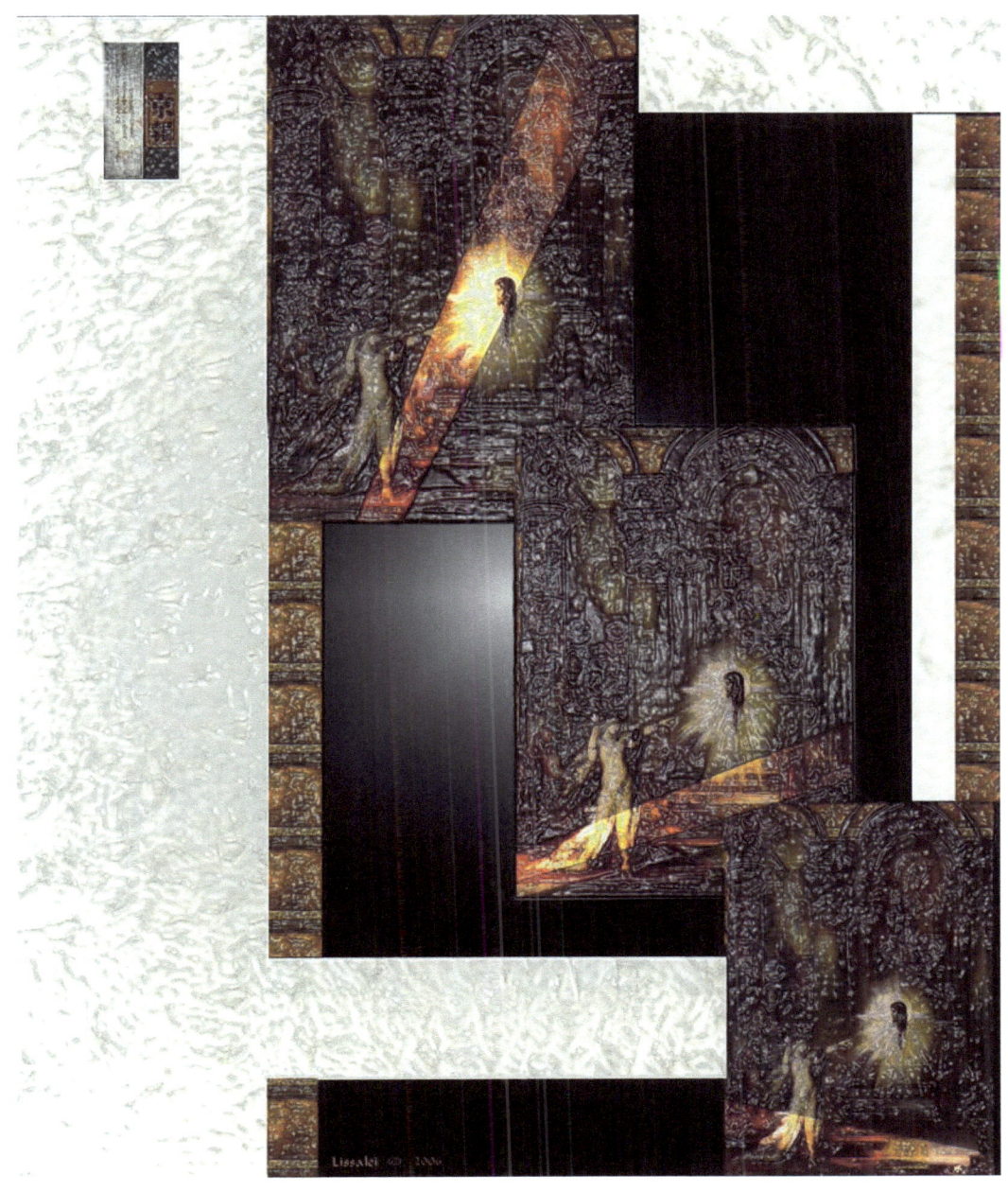

Retribution

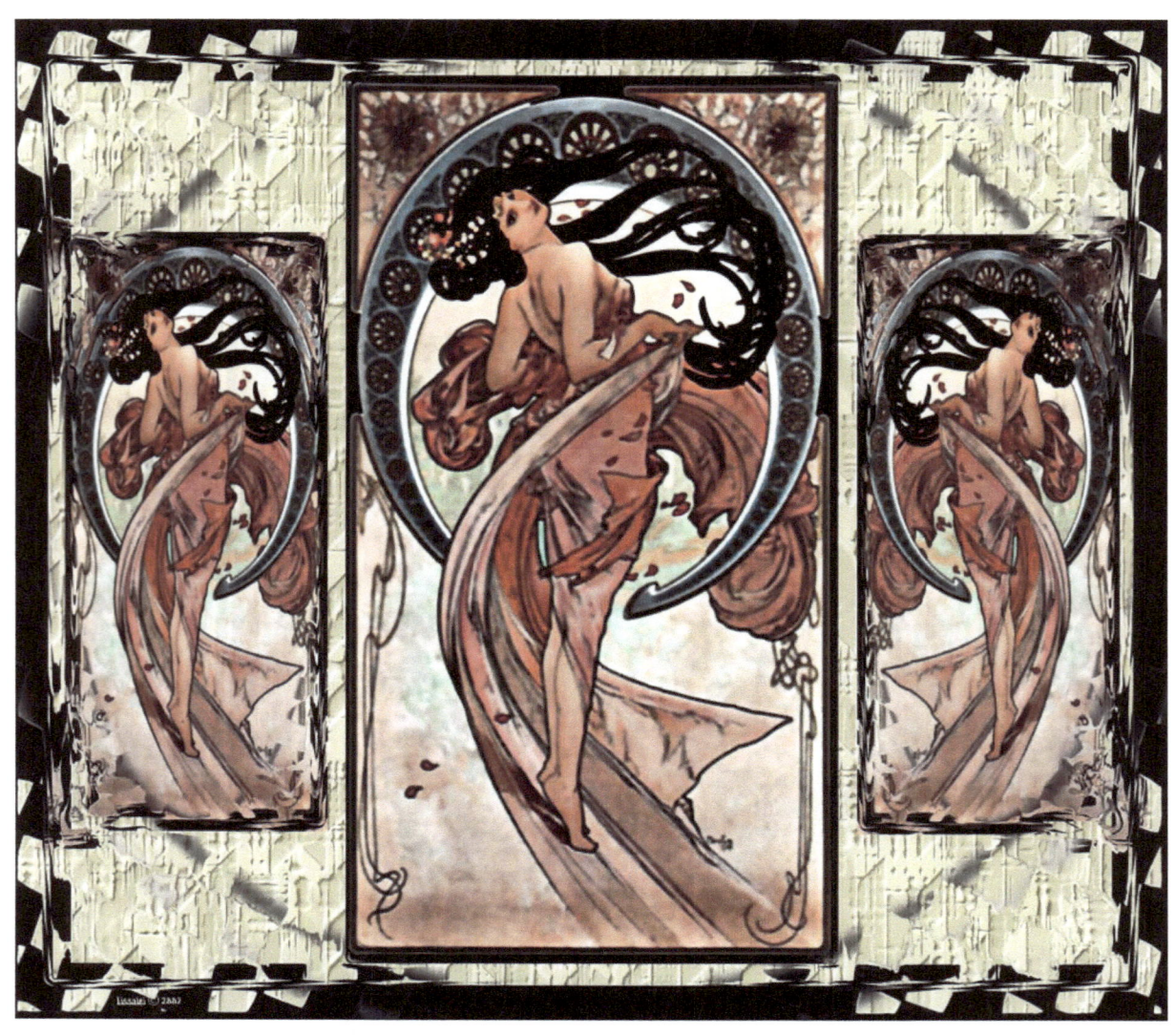

Ballo Da Donna

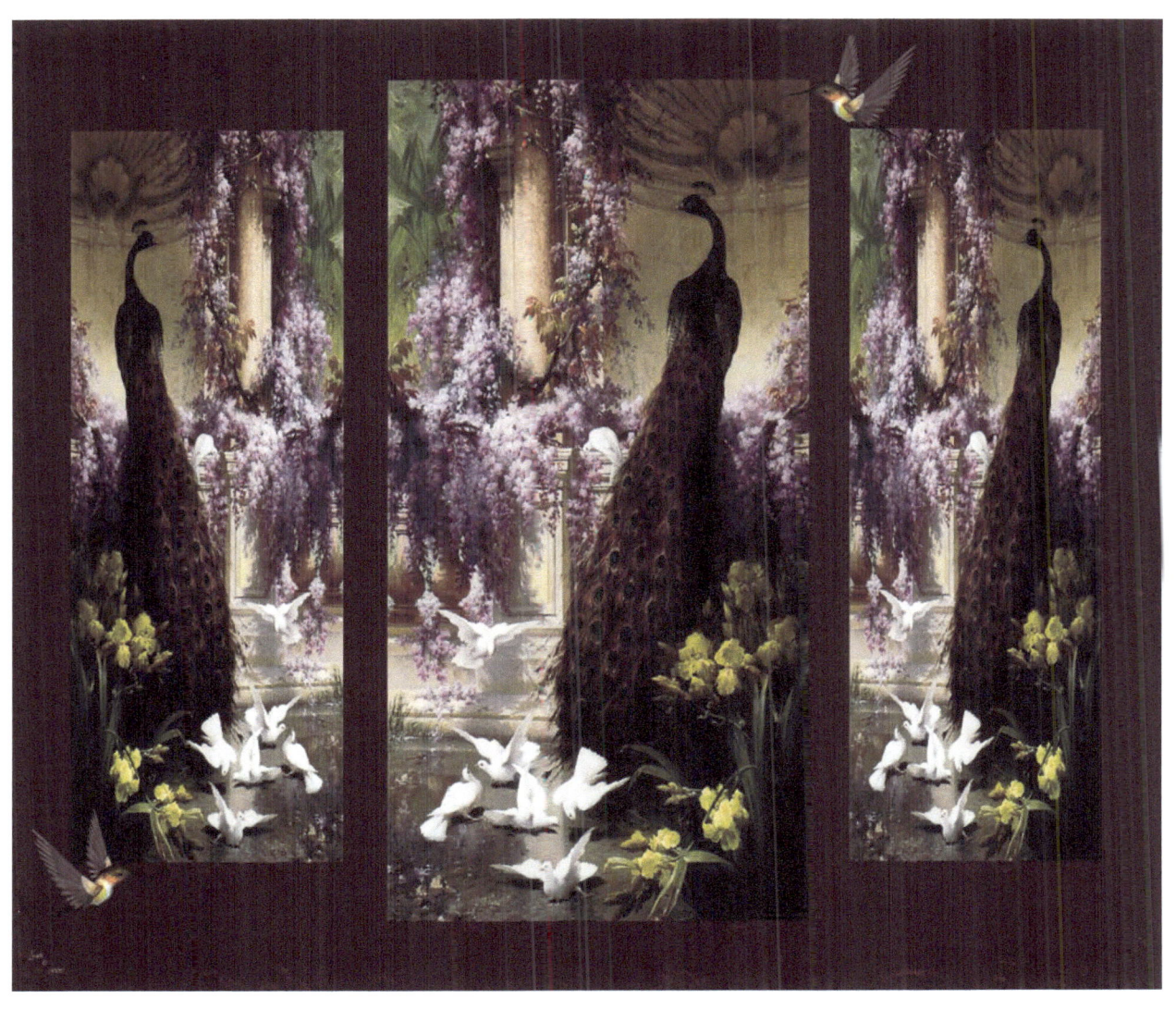

Exotica

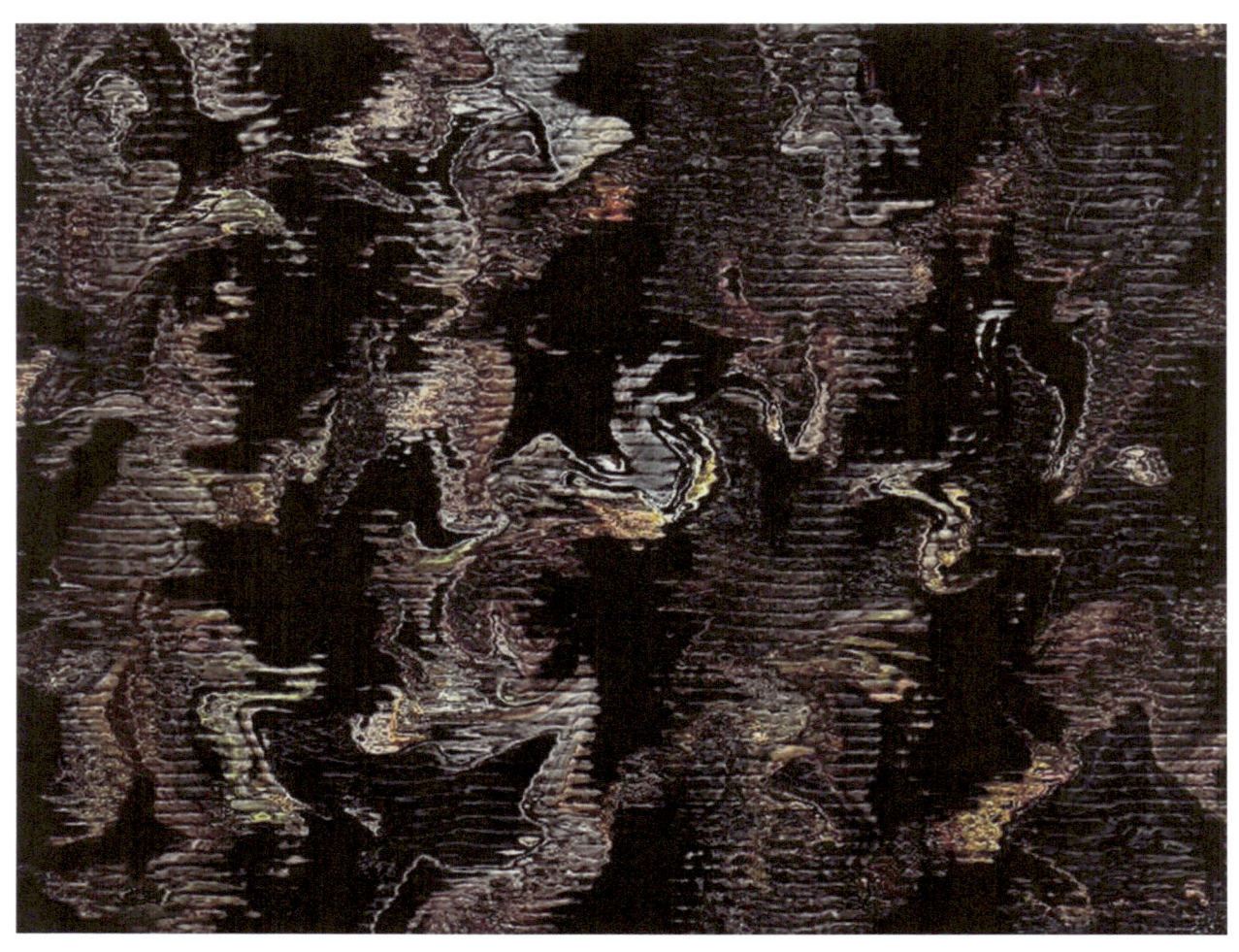

Darker

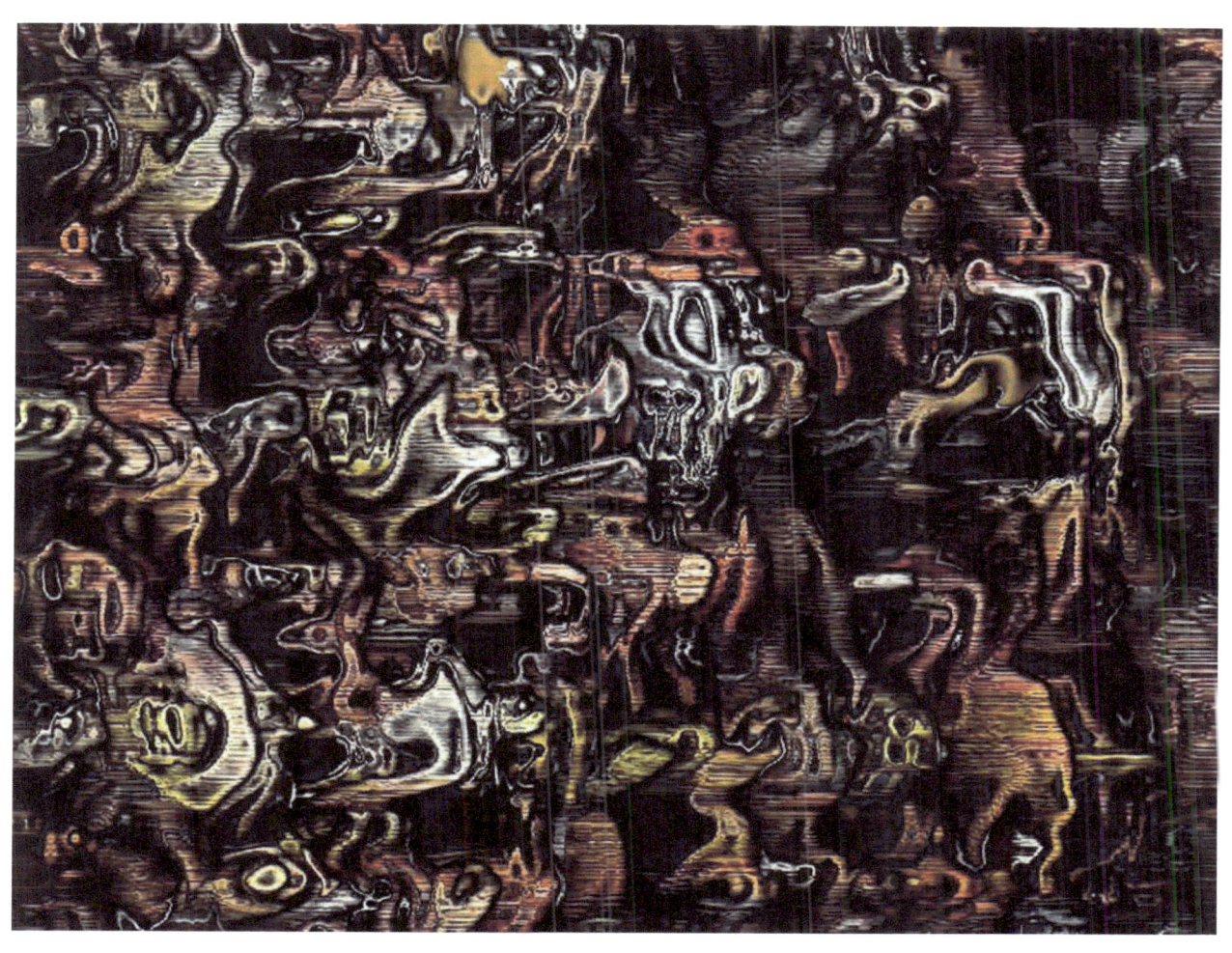

Distracted Abstract

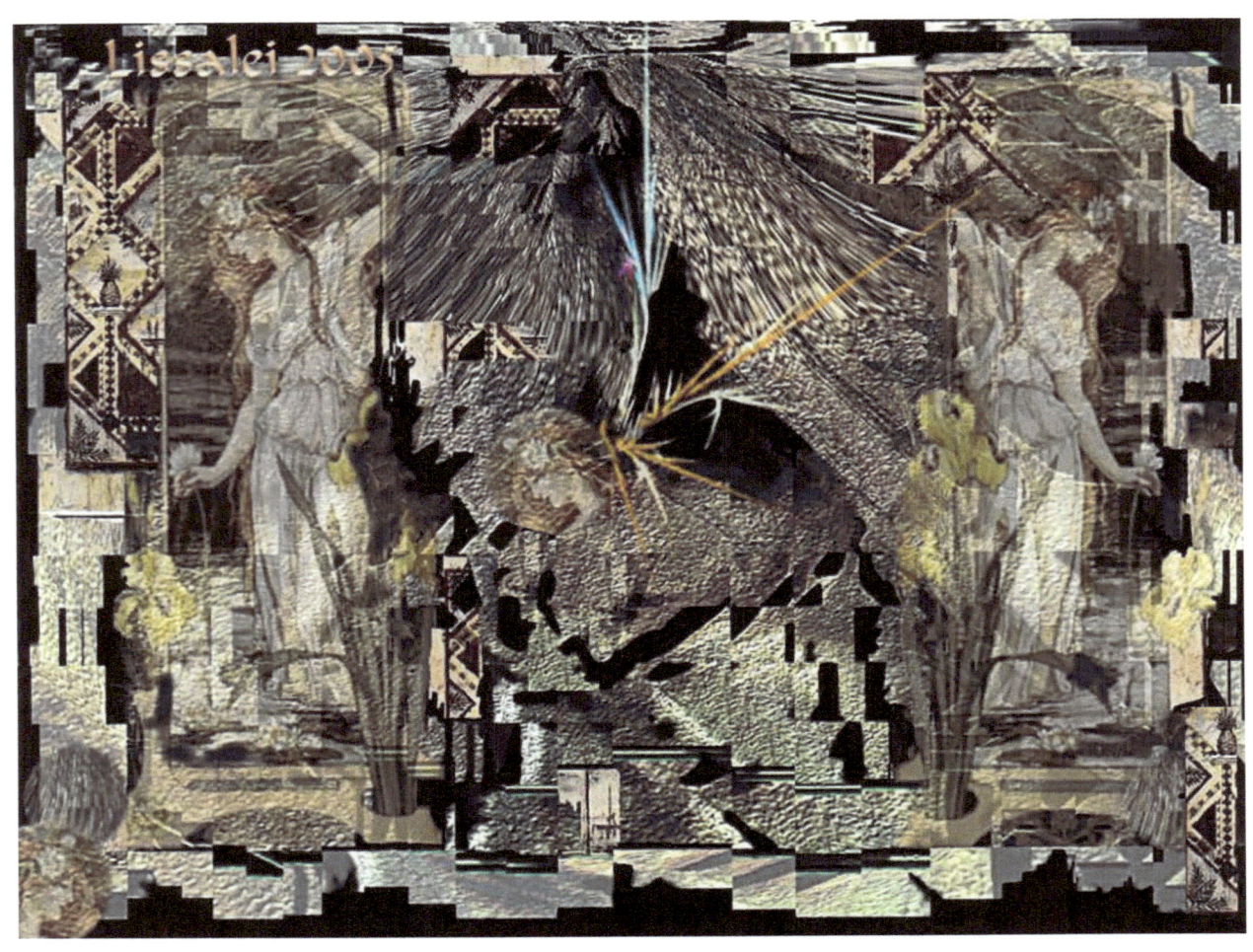

Cadenza

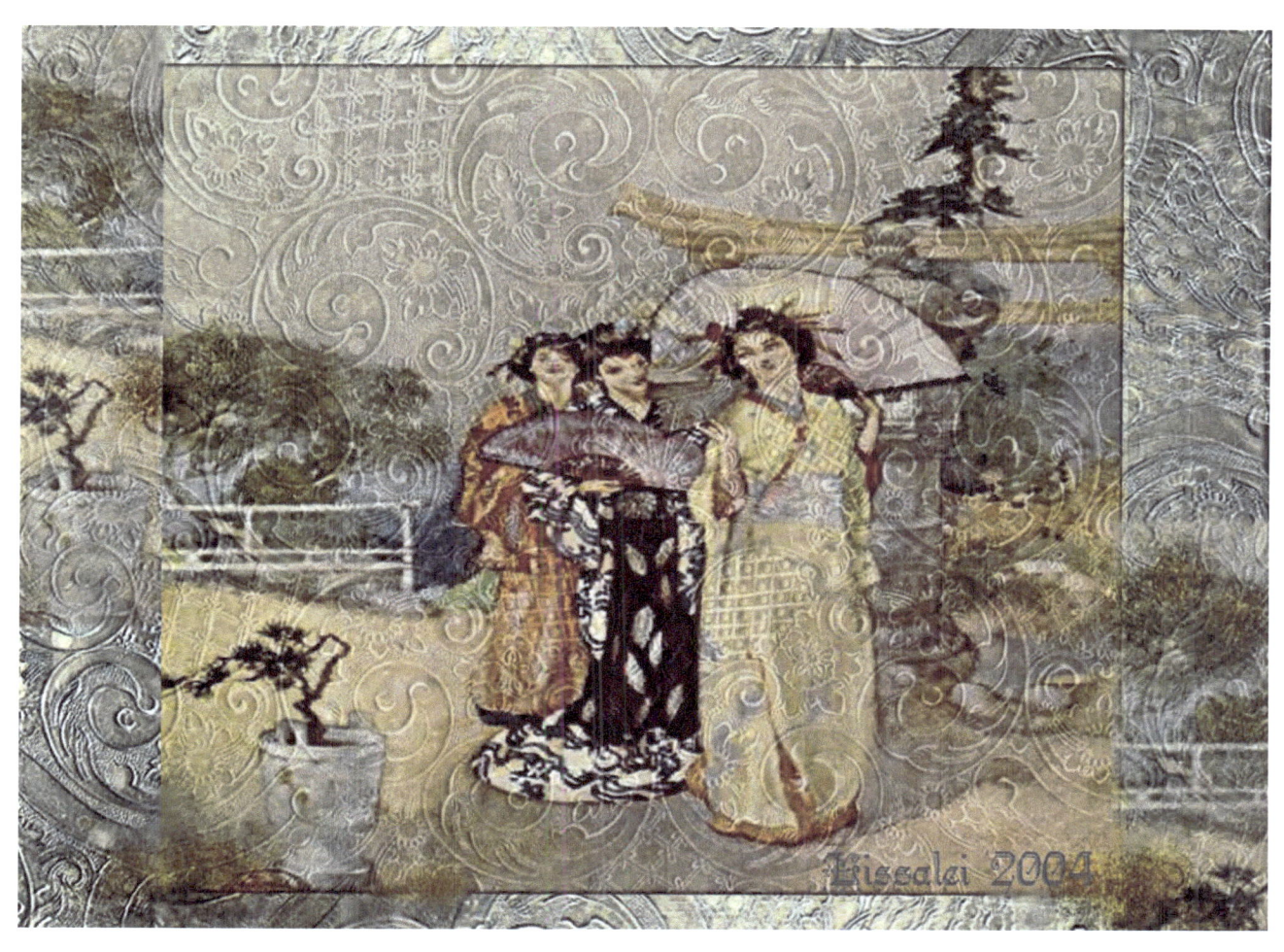

Afternoon Delight

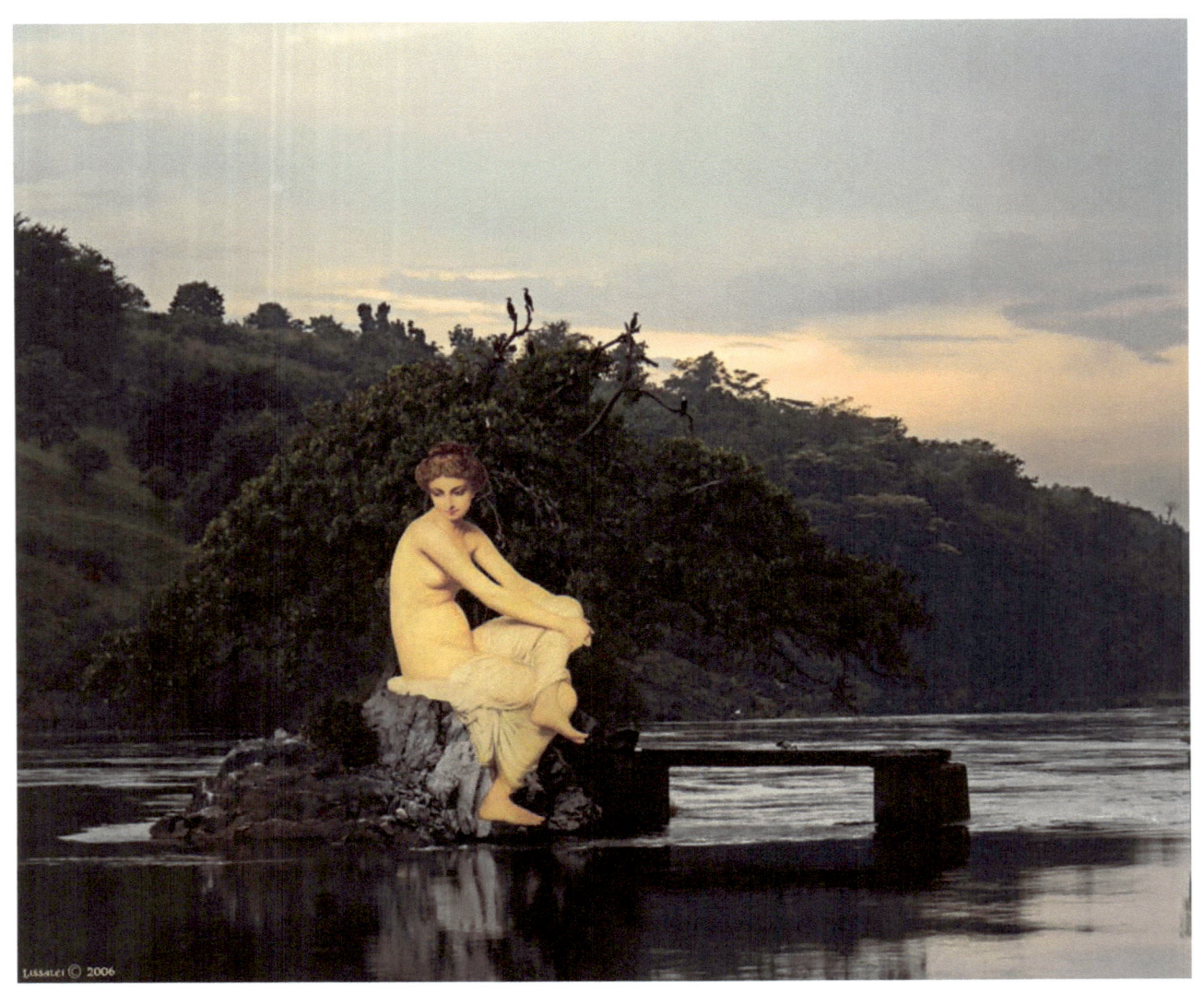

Serenity

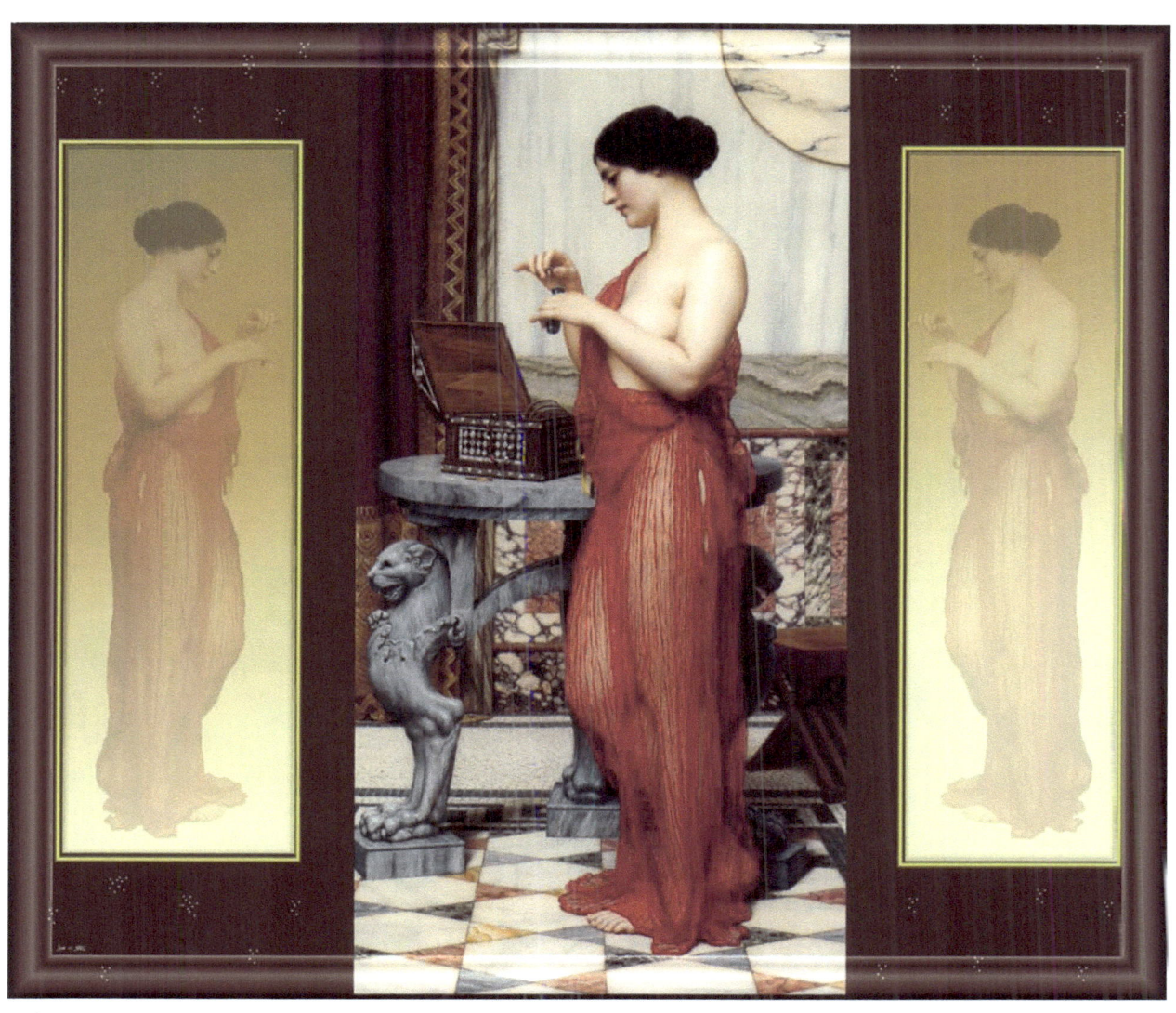

New Perfume

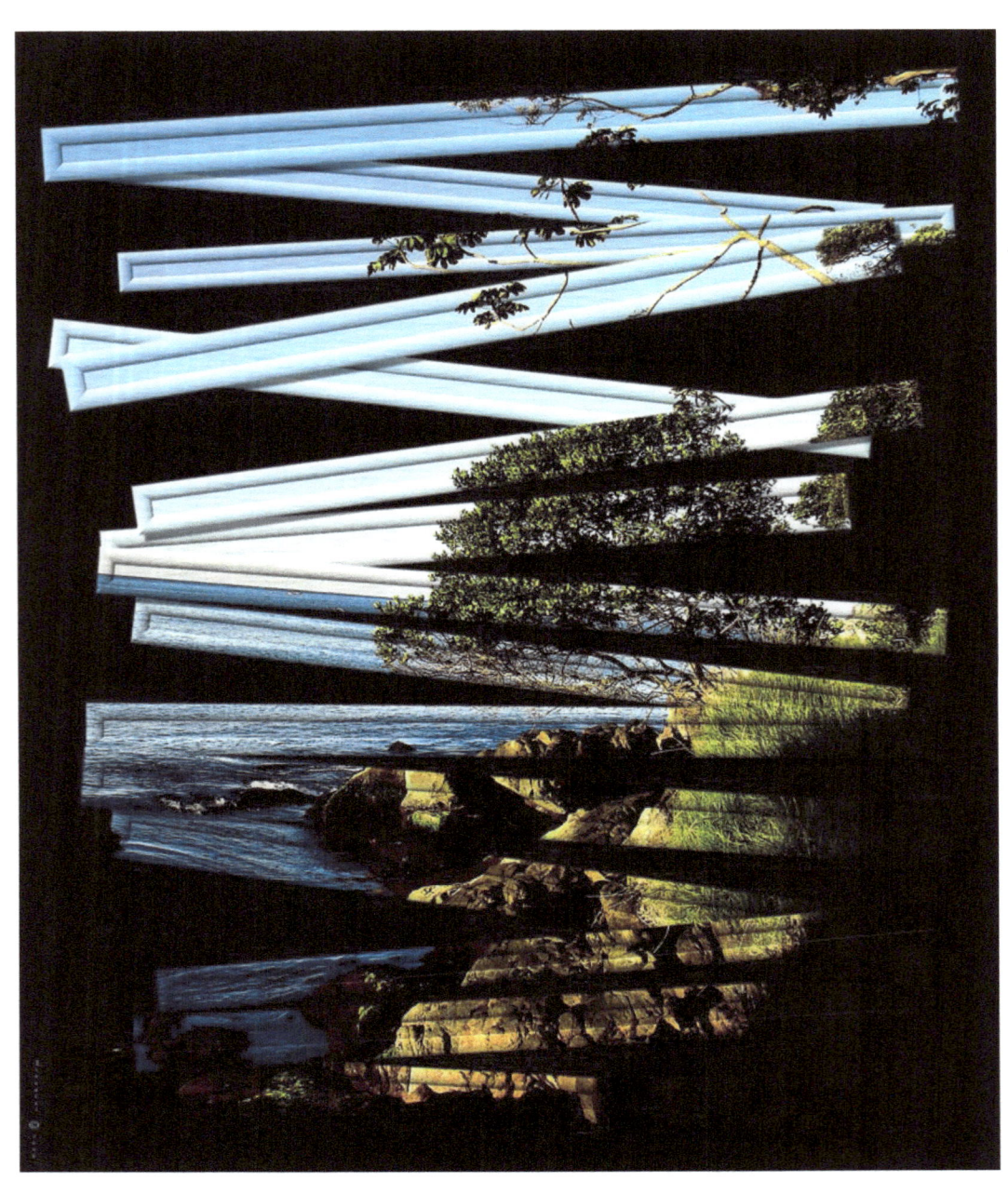

Perspective (Chopsticks)

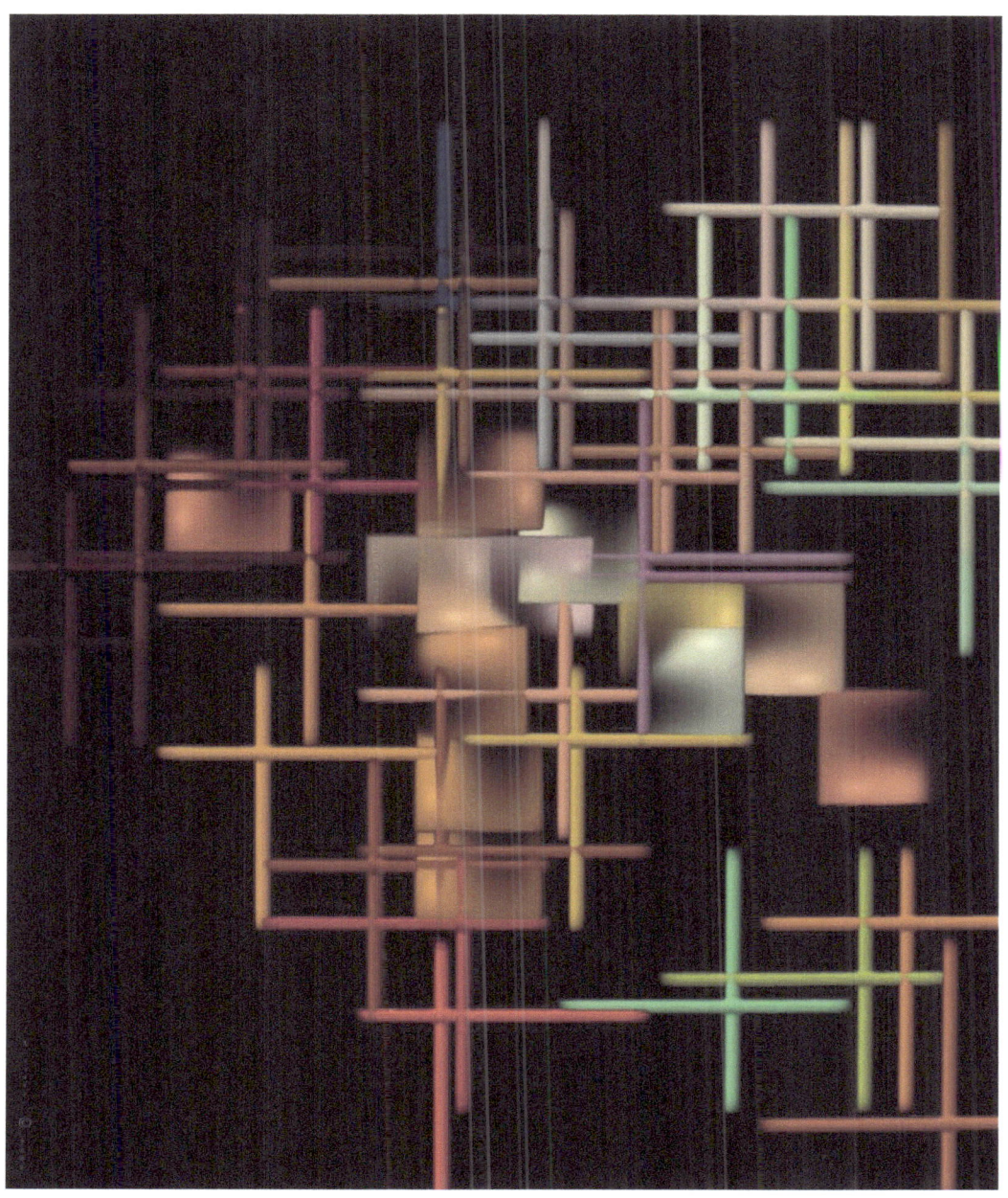

Pipes

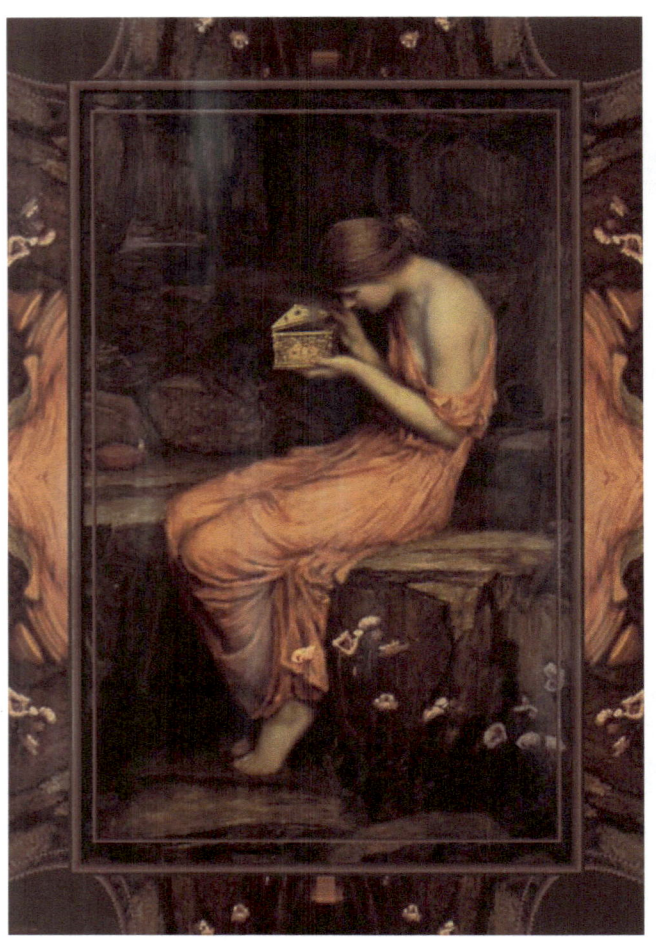

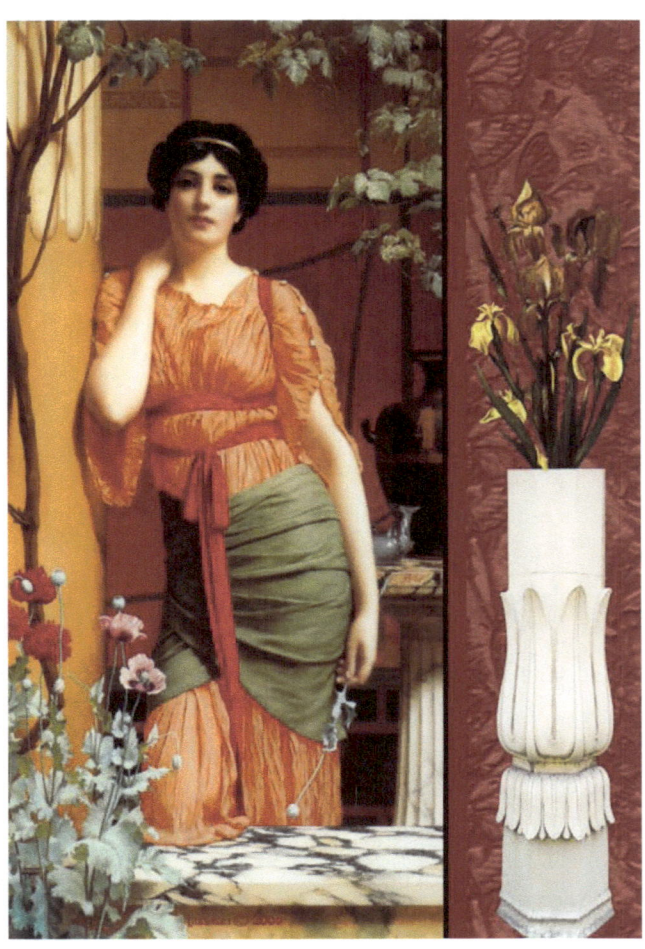

Through the Mists of Time   *Nerissa*

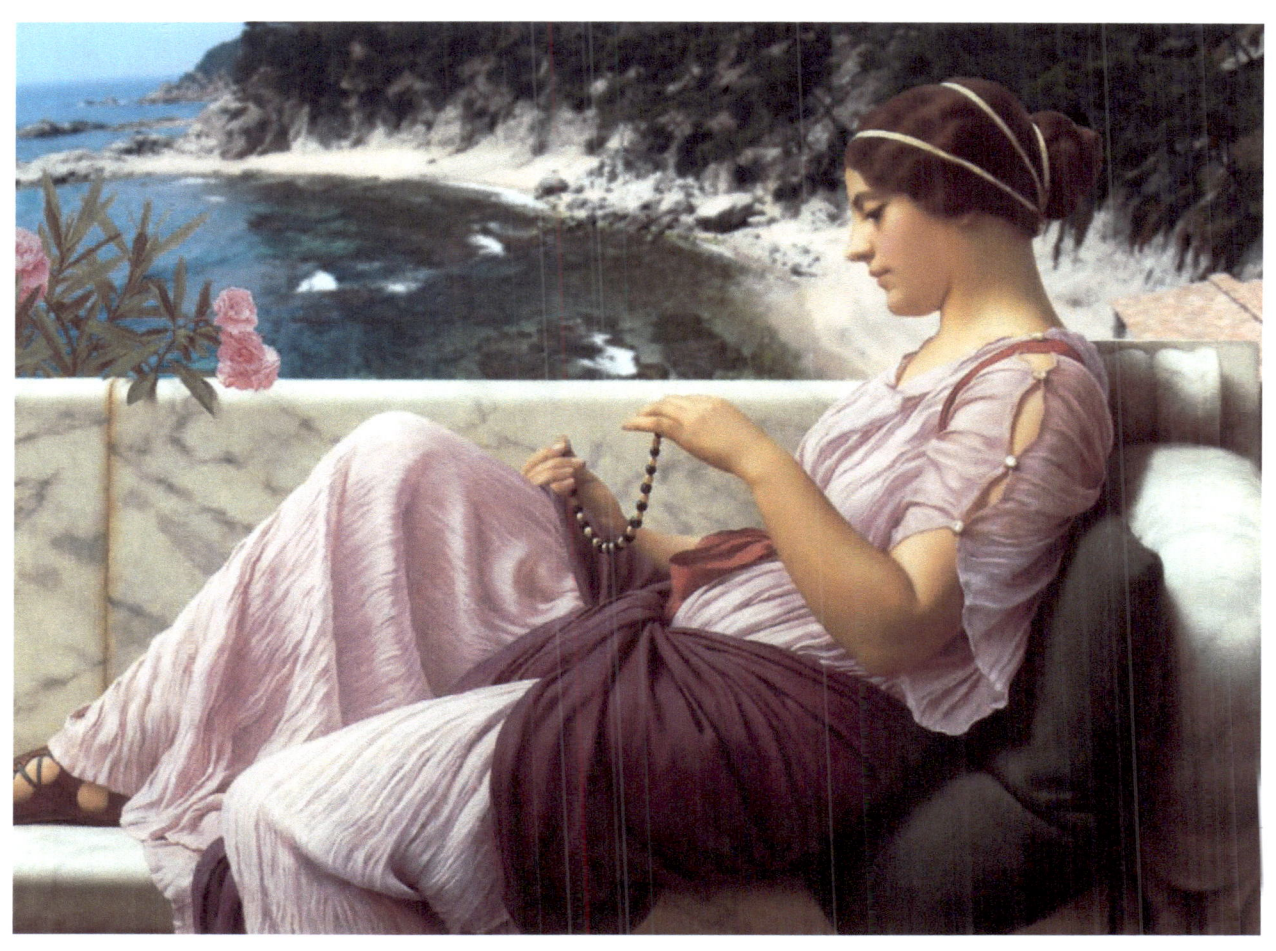

Contemplation

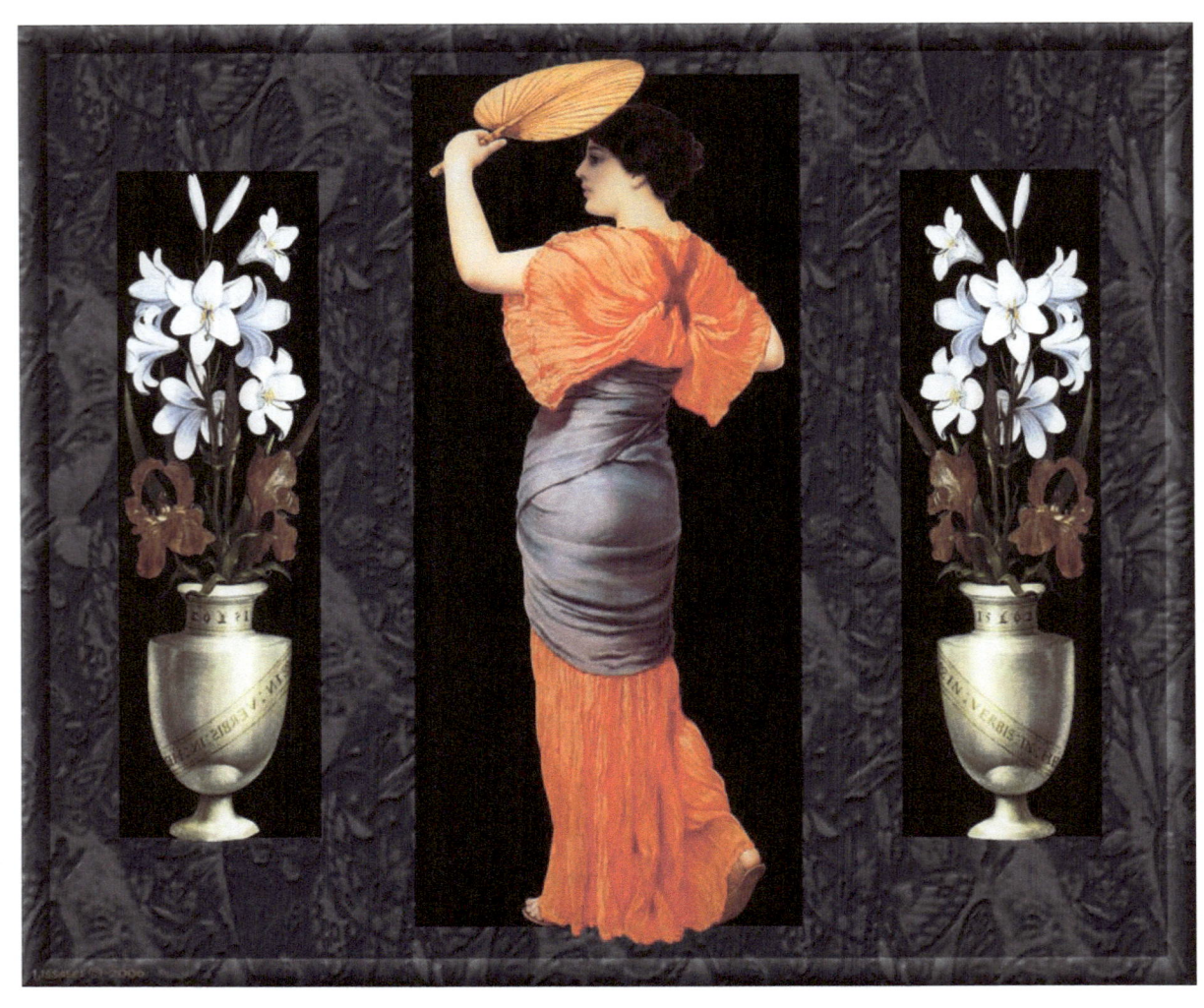

Girl Waiting

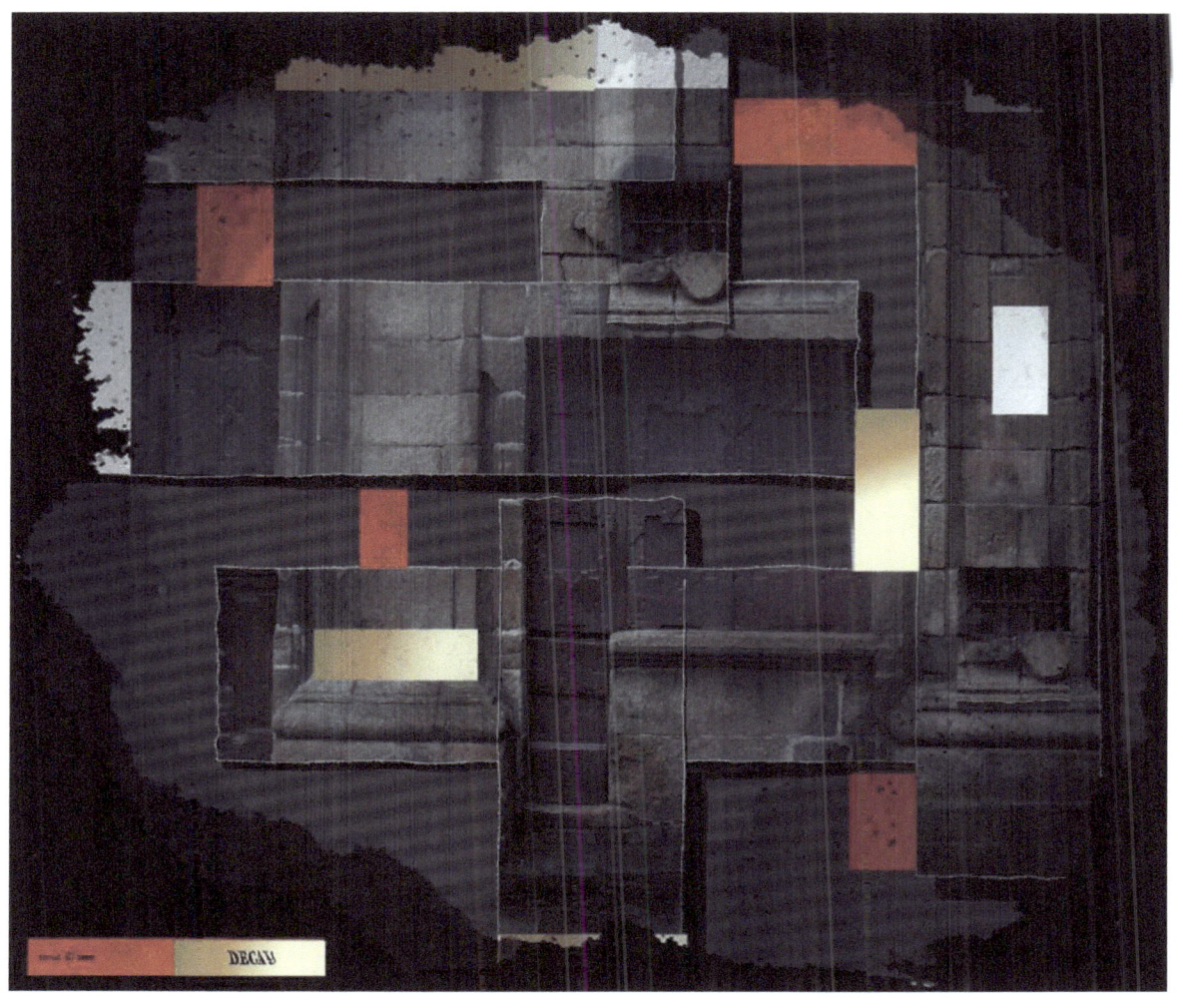

Decay

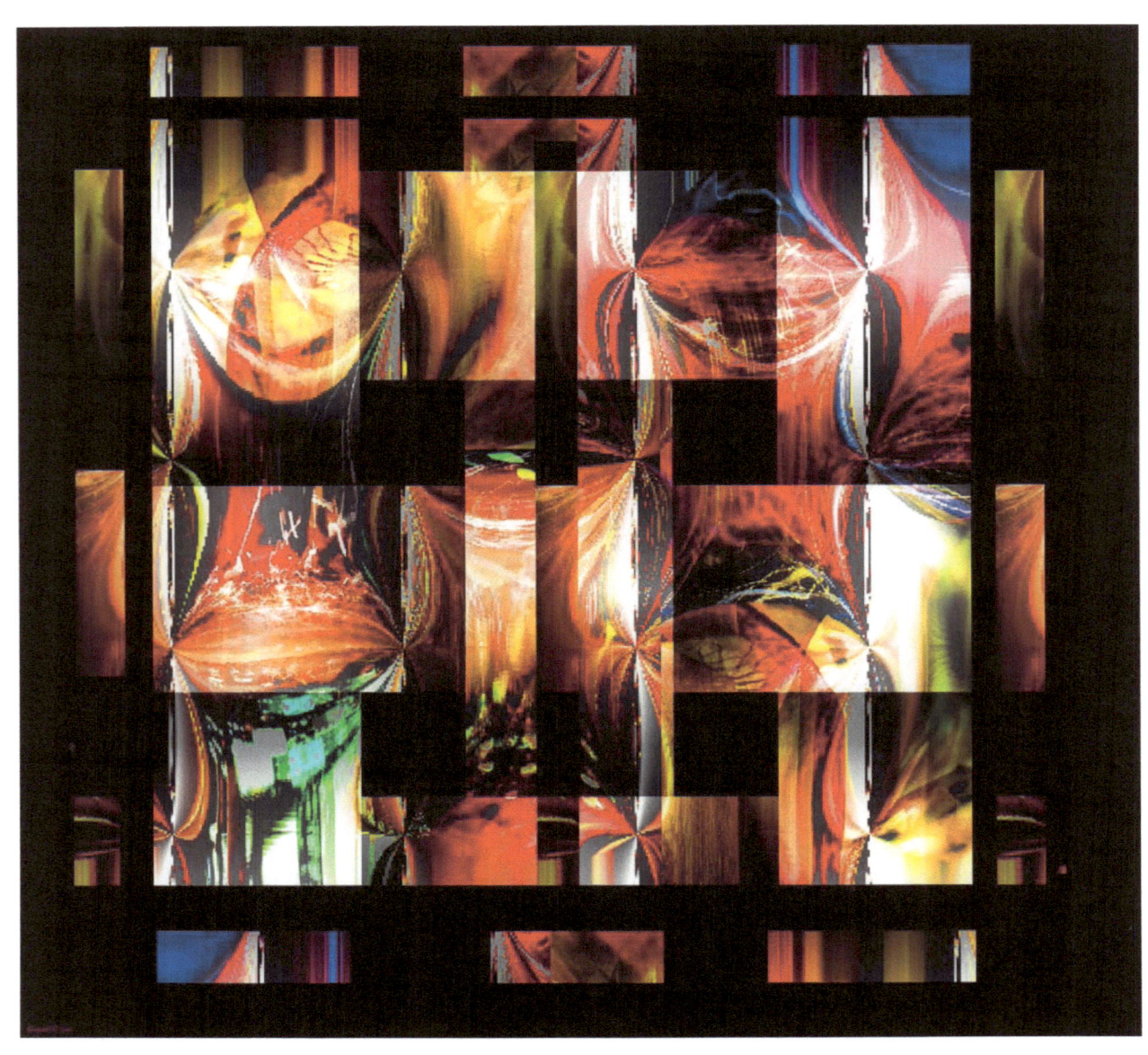

Woven Abstract

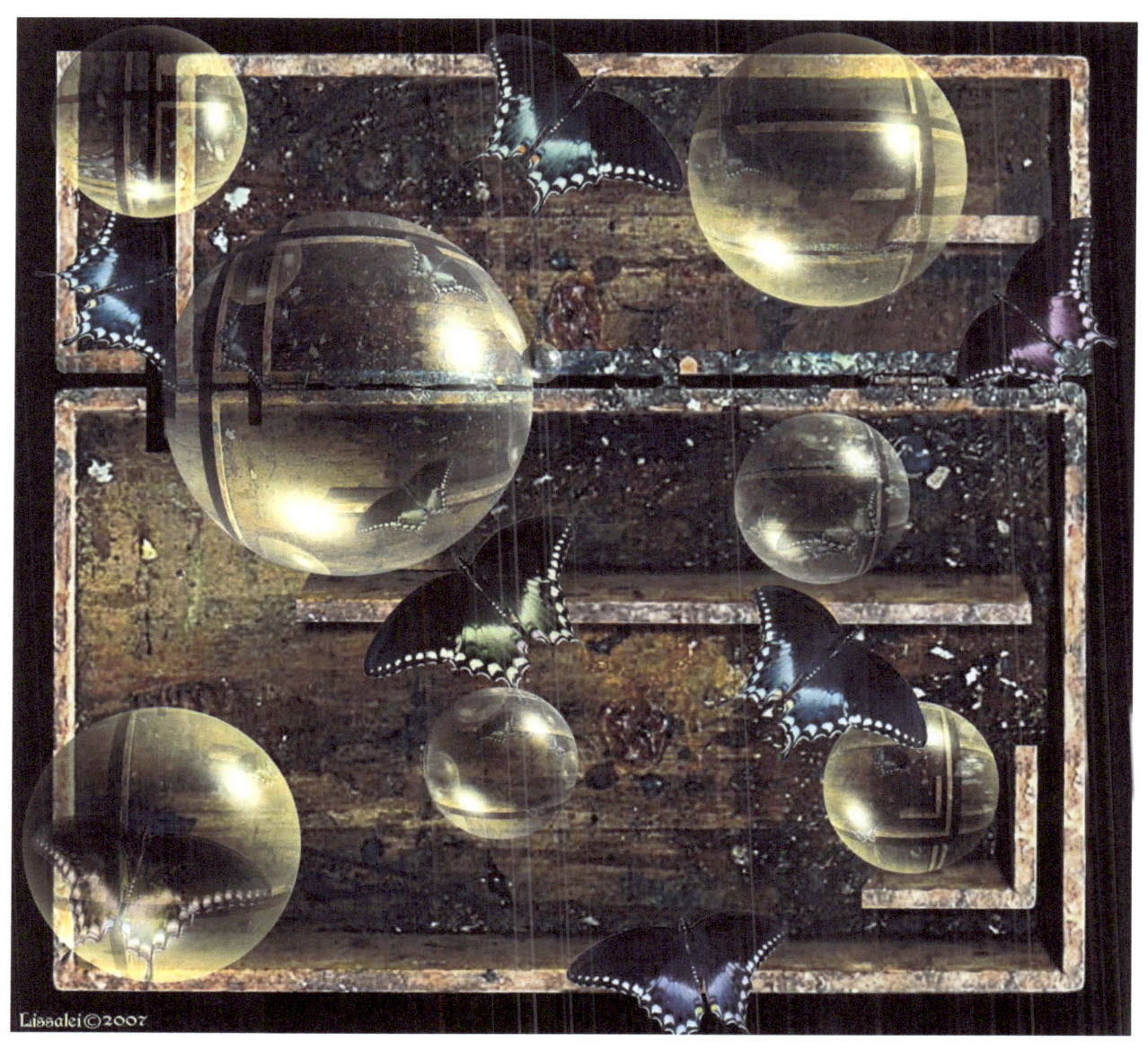

Butterfly Spheres

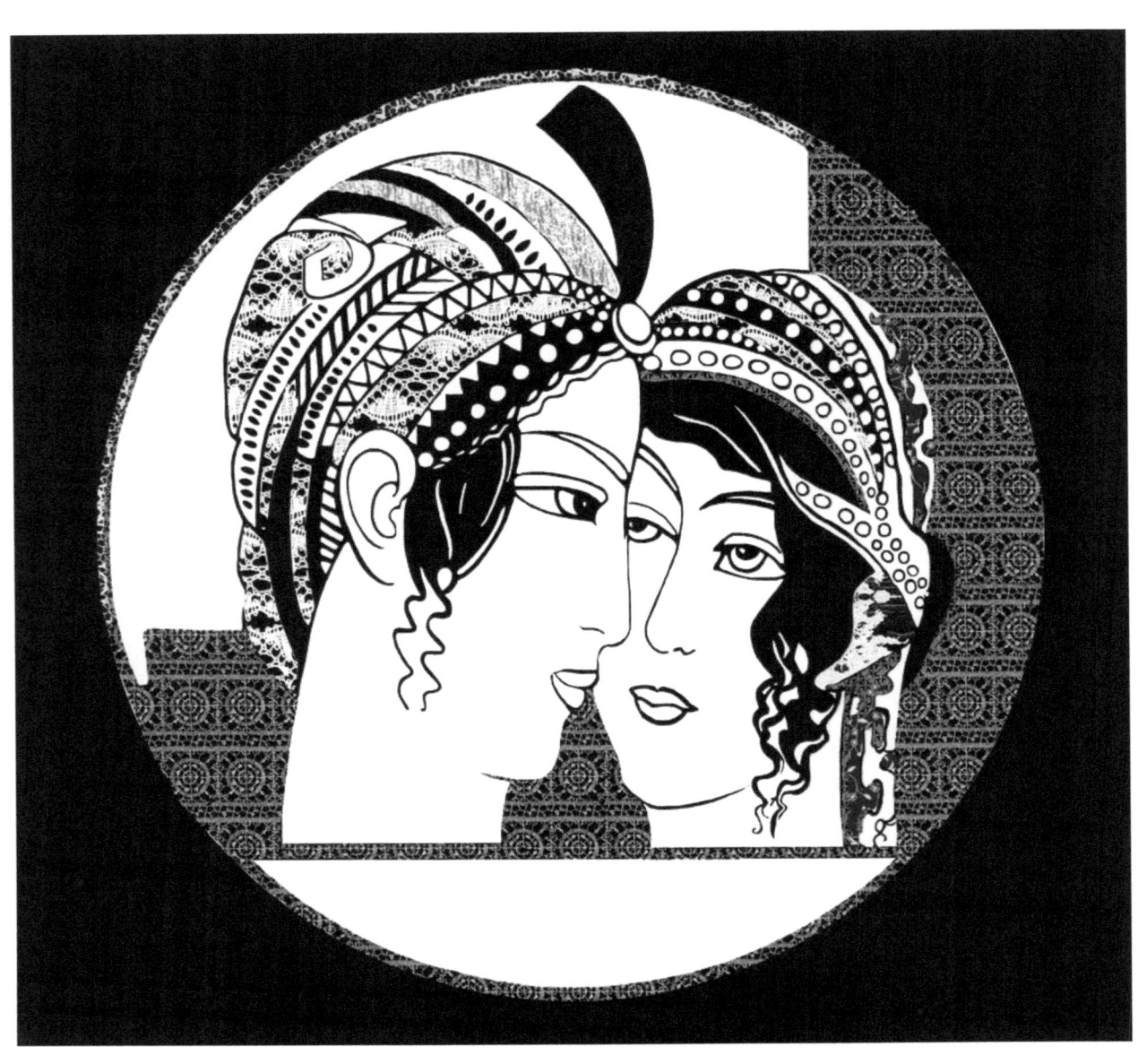

Art Deco Number 2

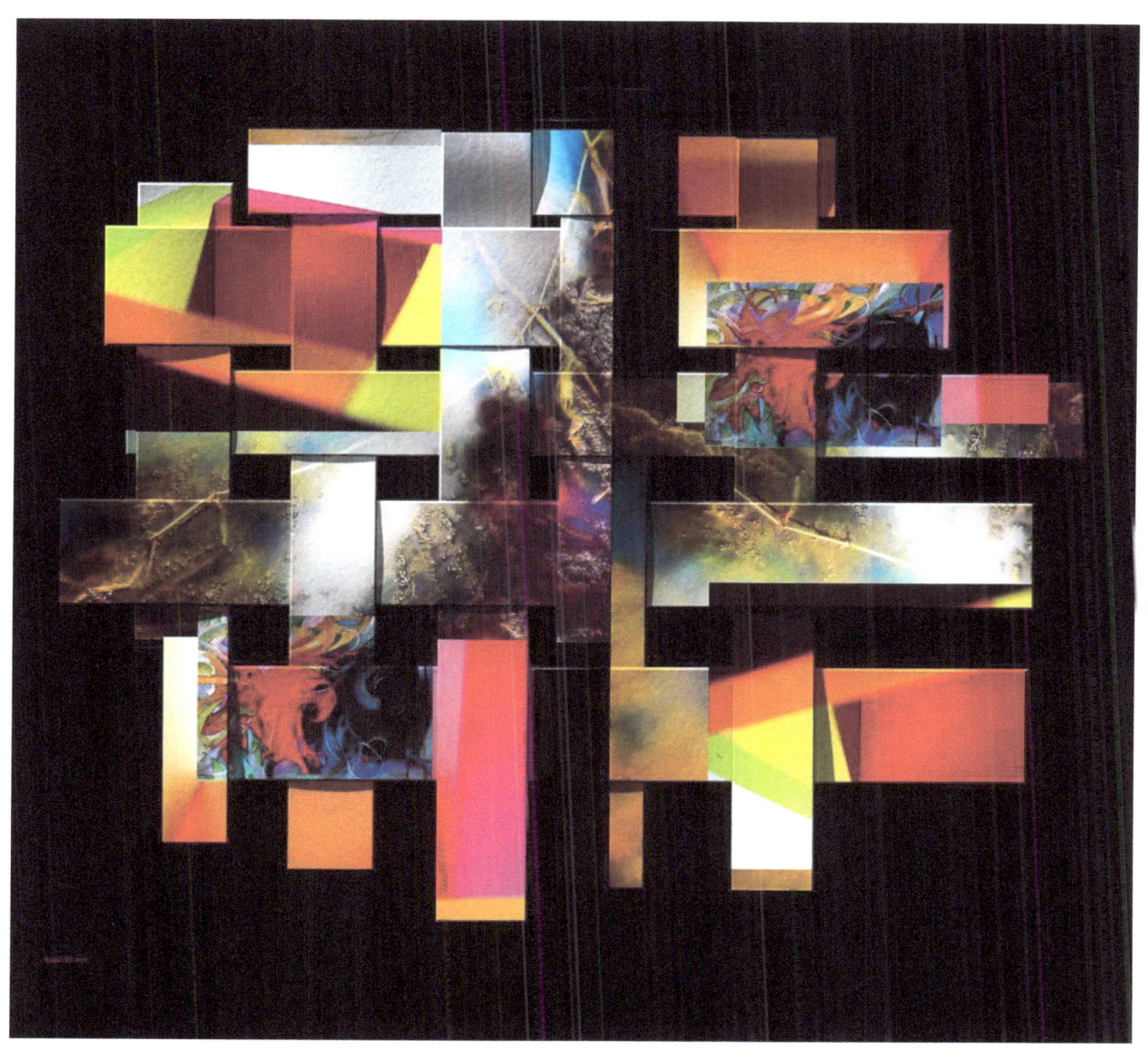

Weaving

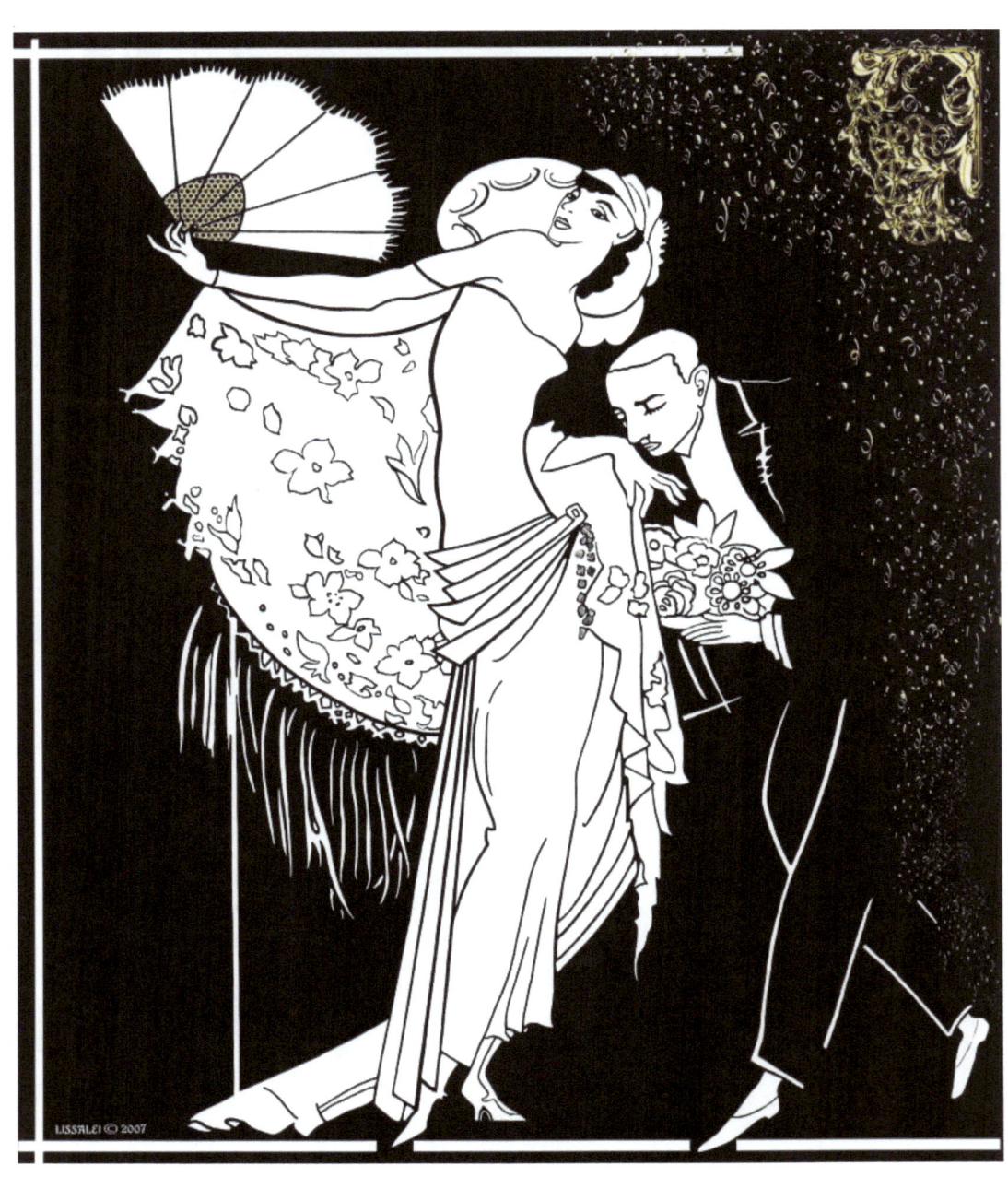

Golden Moments

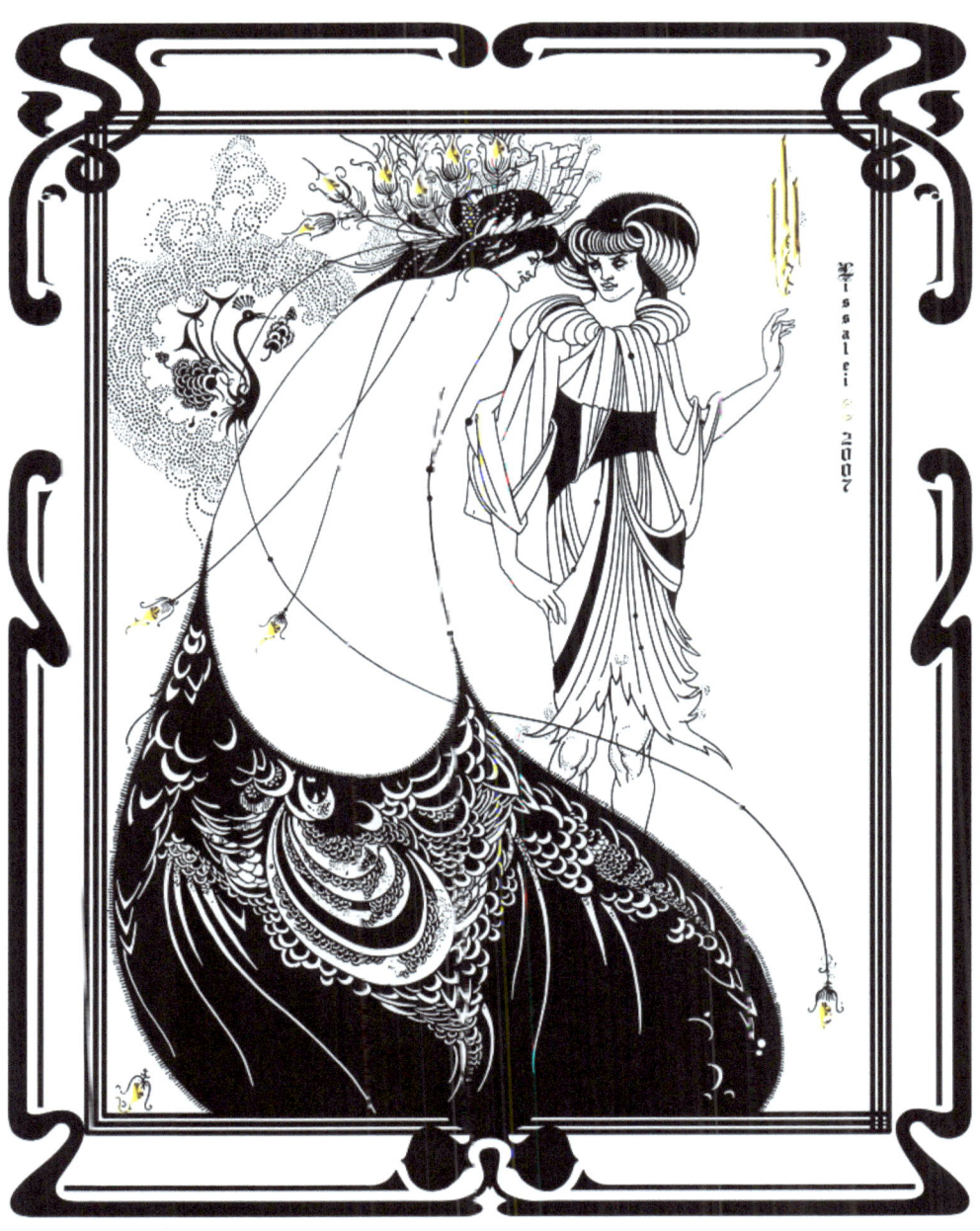

Peacock Skirt

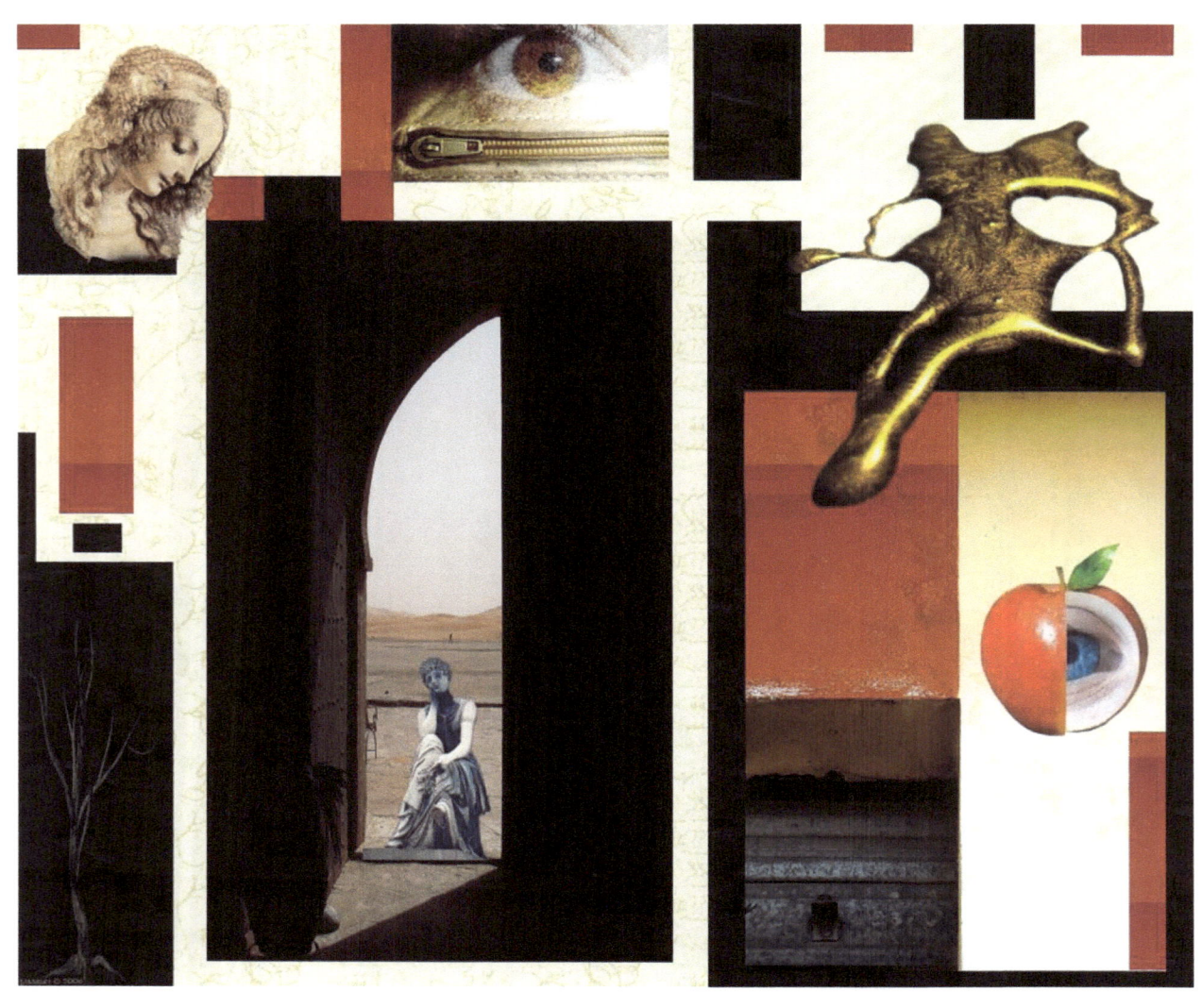

Distracted Eyes

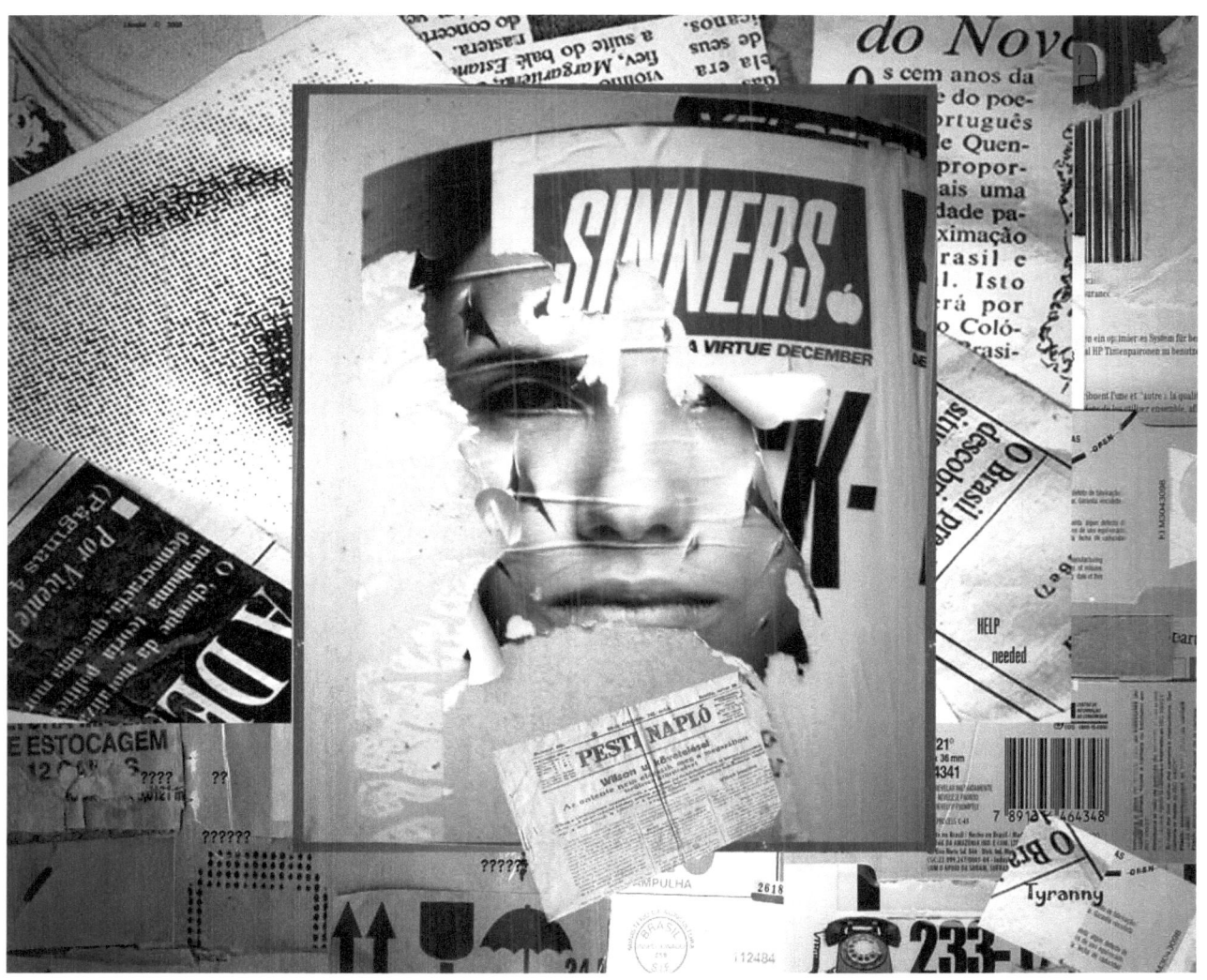

In the News

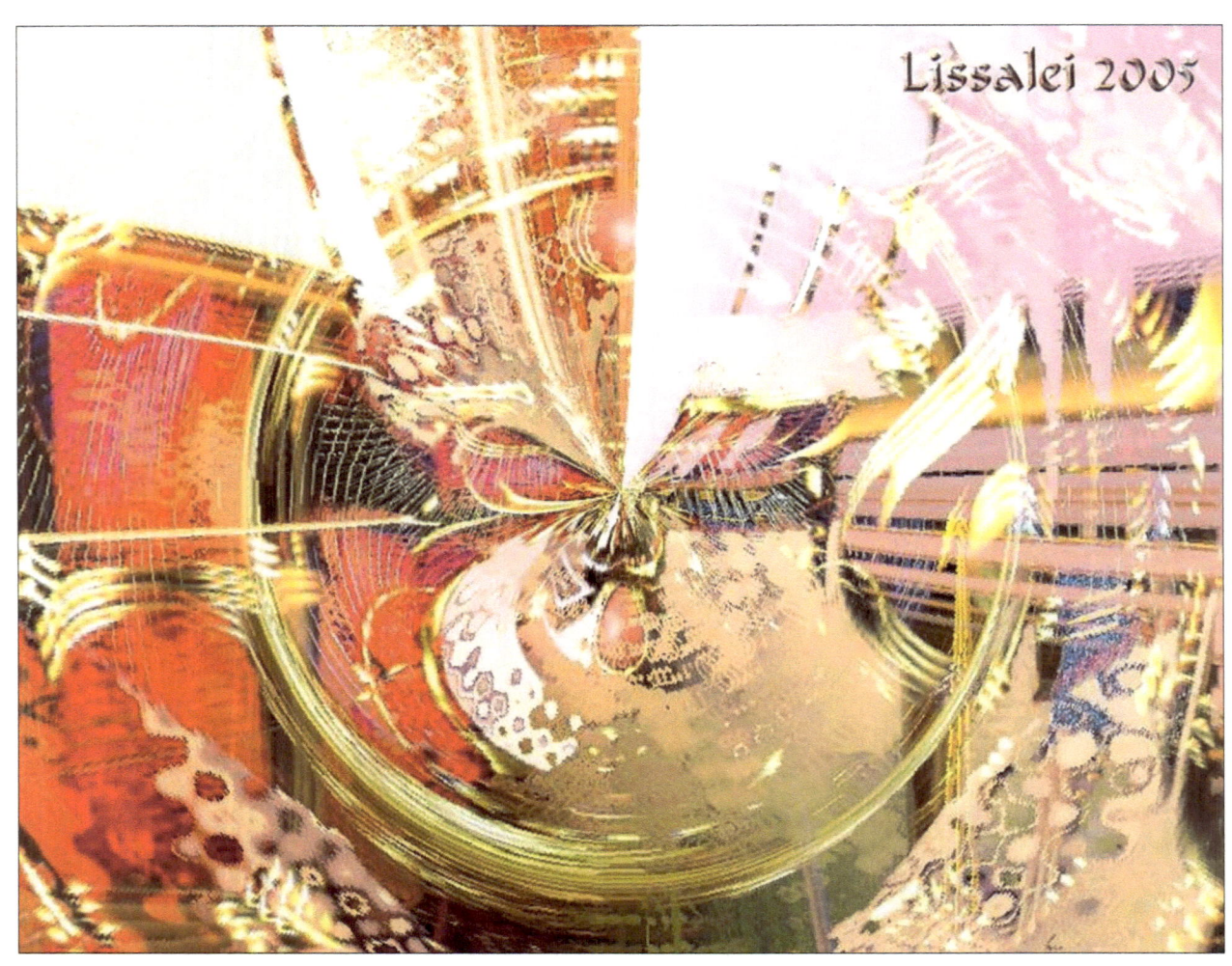

Soft Fusion

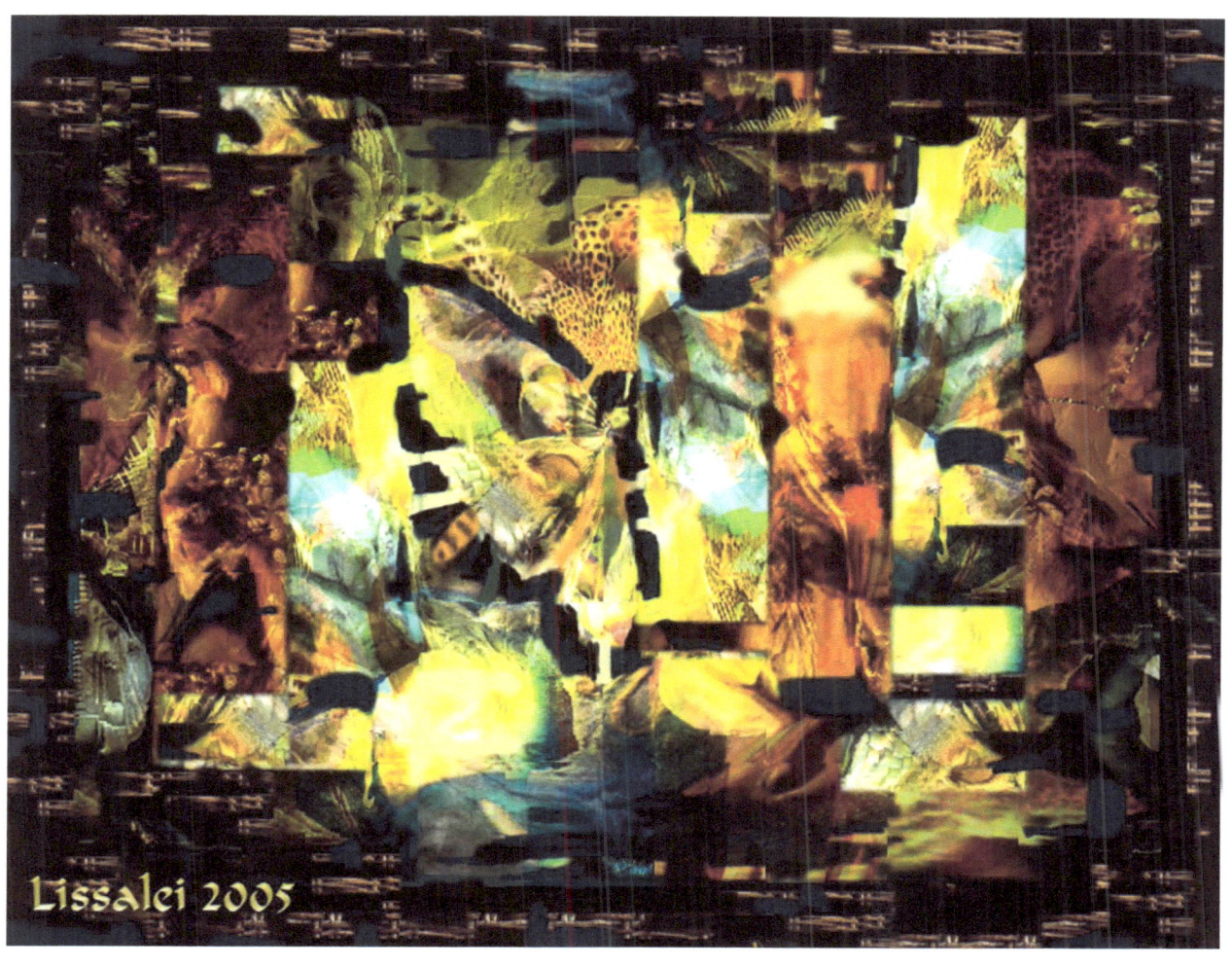

Instant Karma

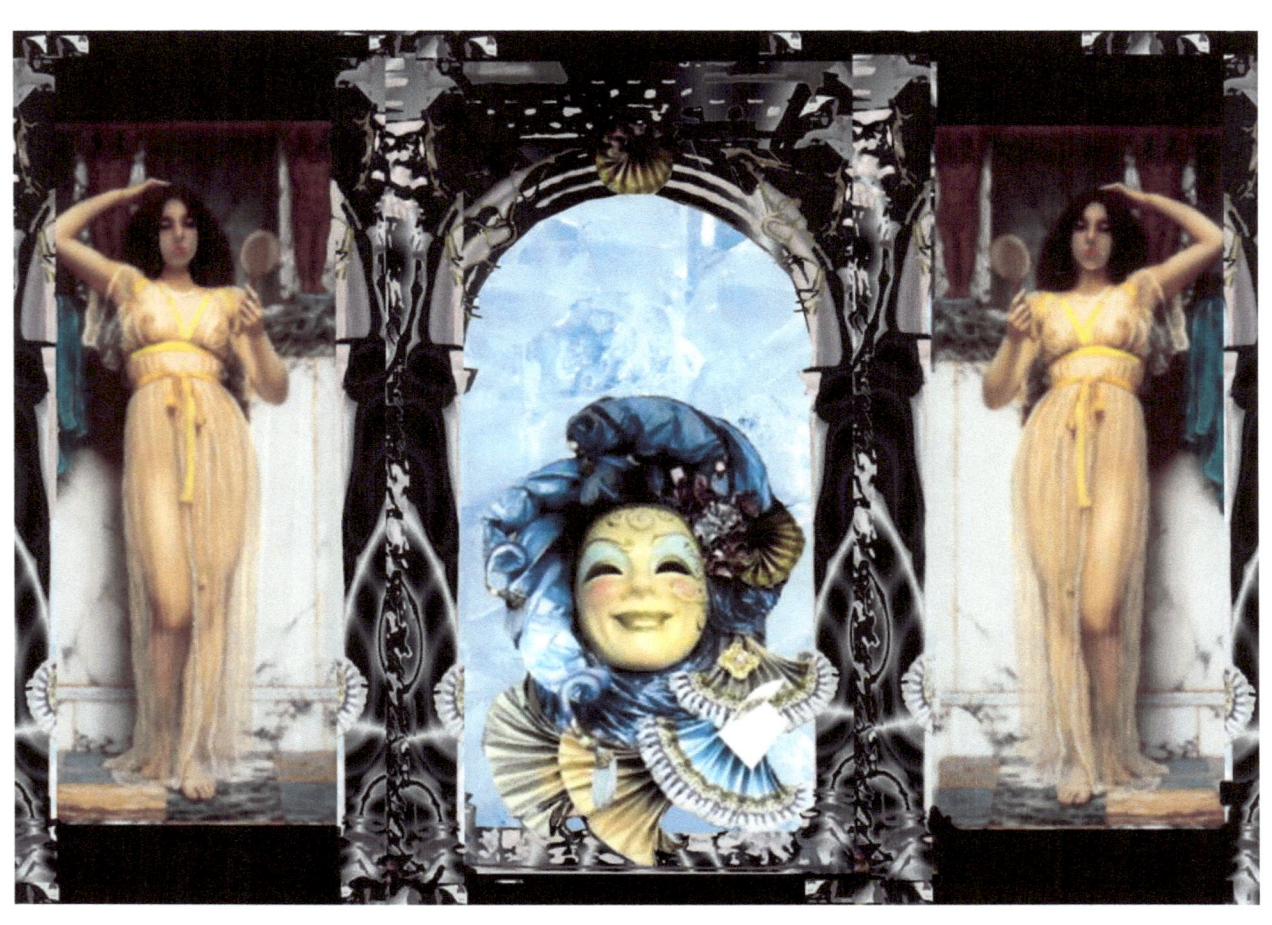

Venetian Mask

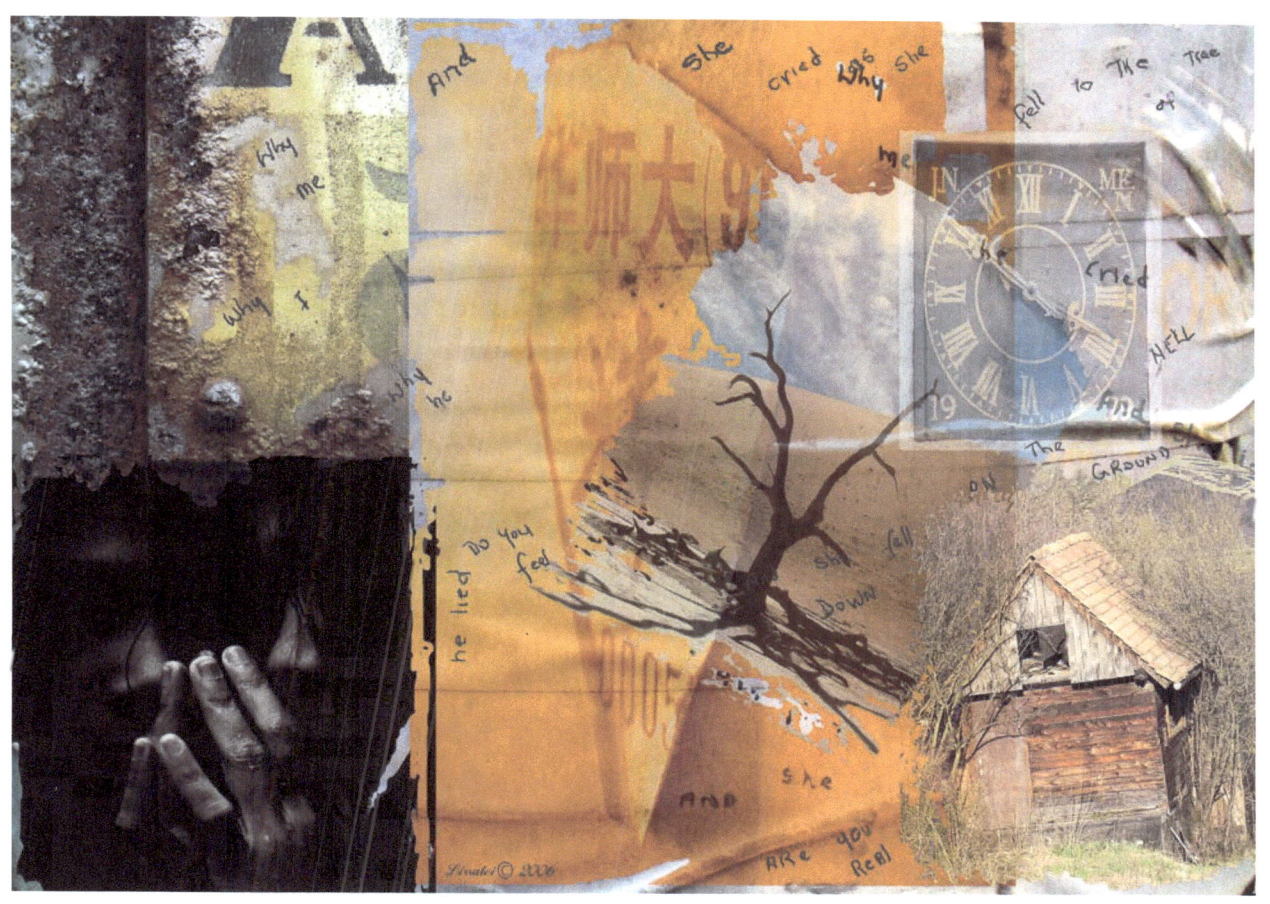

Death Tree

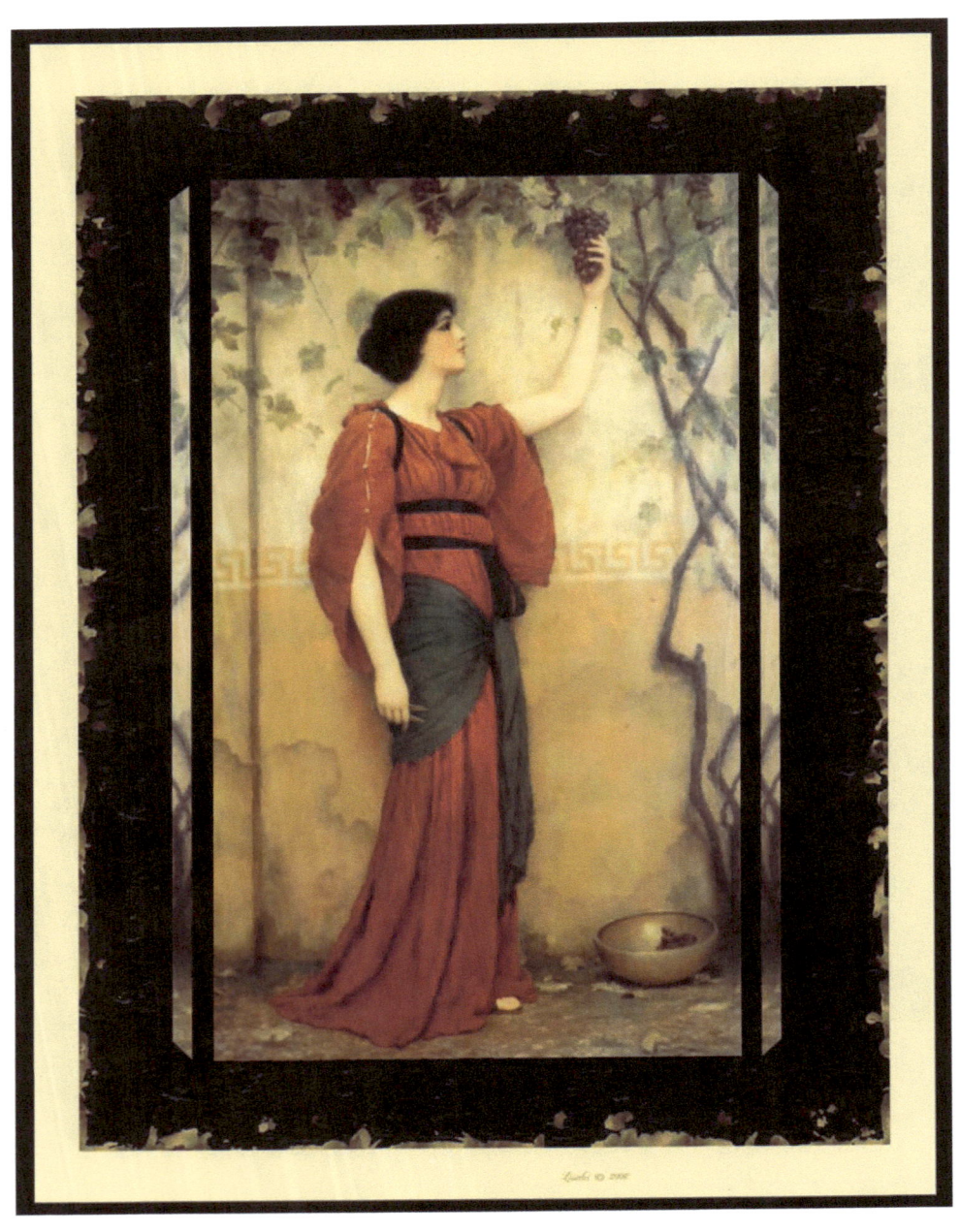

A Sweet Treat

Butterfly Spheres

The text for this book was set in ParmaPetit, designed by Manfred Klein Fonteria. The display type is Bavand.

This book was designed by Walton Mendelson, 12on14.com, for One-Off Press, and printed by CreateSpace, a division of Amazon.com.